CONCILIUM

Religion in the Eighties

CONCILIUM

Concilium 155 (5/1982): Fundamental Theology

IS BEING HUMAN A CRITERION OF BEING CHRISTIAN?

Edited by
Jean-Pierre Jossua
and
Claude Geffré

English Language Editor
Marcus Lefébure

T. & T. CLARK LTD.
Edinburgh

THE SEABURY PRESS
New York

May 1982
T. & T. Clark Ltd., 36 George Street, Edinburgh EH2 2LQ
ISBN: 0 567 30035 8

The Seabury Press, 815 Second Avenue, New York, NY 10017
ISBN: 0 8164 2386 5

Library of Congress Catalog Card No.: 81-85842

Printed in Scotland by William Blackwood & Sons Ltd., Edinburgh

Concilium: Monthly except July and August
Subscriptions 1982: UK and Rest of the World £27·00, postage and handling included; USA and Canada, all applications for subscriptions and enquiries about *Concilium* should be addressed to The Seabury Press, 815 Second Avenue, New York, NY 10017, USA.

CONTENTS

Editorial

The Human Factor — the Criterion of Initial Christian Existence

WHAT IS the meaning, the value and the importance of human existence as such, that is, in everyday life, in politics and in culture, for Christians? This is a fundamental question that arises again and again. It is perhaps implied in Christian practice rather than explicitly asked by professional theologians, but this does not mean that it does not for this reason have any theological overtones.

Ought we, for example, to say that the more authentically and completely human we are, the more Christian we must be—even if our humanity is not the only criterion of our Christianity? Or ought we rather to insist that every advance made in human life is an opportunity to deepen our grasp of the Gospel—and vice versa? It is possible to maintain, in the perspective of the incarnation, that the most sublime realities involved in the 'kingdom of God' are bound to take place within human existence, so that, in carrying out these tasks, we are not set at a distance from God, but are rather made intermediaries so that others may encounter him? This would demand what Péguy called 'the maximum from God and the maximum from man'. It would mean that we would be acting as protagonists of a 'humanist' Christianity—we do not necessarily say of a 'Christian humanism'—as opposed to what could be called a 'monastic' type of Christianity.

By 'monastic Christianity', we mean here a Christianity which results in a flight from the world as an obstacle—because of the human body or because of sin—to life led according to the Gospel and a renunciation of certain important aspects of human life and even of one's own personality, with the aim of finding God. This definition of the 'monastic' ideology clearly does not provide any real answer to the question of the religious life of the Church, although it cannot be denied that calling the 'monastic' ideology into question is bound to have certain repercussions on the Church's religious life.

This debate has preoccupied Christians and it will undoubtedly continue in the Church. In the course of its history, very many different suggestions have been made. What is fundamentally at stake is our understanding of the relationship between the New and the Old Testaments. The latter is so obviously concerned with man's existence on earth. The Old Testament prophets proclaimed a message which had a powerful impact on the political and social life of the people. Jesus' teaching also pointed to this in so far as it was the continuation of the prophetic message and the kingdom of God that he inaugurated led, among other things, to a revolution in individual and social relationships.

In this, an important part is played by the way in which we regard the imminent eschatological expectation on the one hand and the corresponding disappointment of our unfulfilled eschatological hope on the other. Do we have to insist, for example, on this eager expectation, which may deprive our concern for life on this earth of its reality, or should we believe that what the 'kingdom of God', which continues to come about in our lives here on earth, offers to us every day should be received by us through the medium of our lives as men and women and in a human history which goes on indefinitely?

This question has so many different aspects and is so full of pitfalls that it is extremely complex. On the other hand, however, if we opt for a 'humanist' interpretation of Christianity—and this is what we have done in this issue of *Concilium*—it can be seen as a question which calls for a frank acceptance of its paradoxical aspects and a resistance to the temptation to change this 'humanist' emphasis in Christianity into a system.

This is, in broad outline, the structure of this issue of *Concilium*. In the first part, we have tried to eliminate some of the pitfalls that we feel stand in the way of progress. It would certainly have been impossible to ask directly what the 'human' factor really is and what Christian existence or the 'specifically' Christian element is. Questions of this kind can only be answered in the whole of this issue of the journal. It is, however, possible to clarify certain terms.

The first of these terms that comes to mind is 'humanism', even if it is used only in its adjectival form and in the limited sense of 'authentically human', as it is here. Peter Eicher has attempted to throw some light on the history of this term and its present significance. He has done so by drawing attention to the important developments in the Western humanist tradition and to Christian thinking in this respect. On the one hand, Eicher points out, Christians have in some ways adapted their own thinking to Western humanist ideas and, on the other, they have also continued to raise their voices in protest against the risk of conformity that is implied in adhering to Western humanism. They have done this by pointing to the distance between humanist ethics on the one hand and the possibility of becoming human provided by the 'humanity of God' on the other.

In the second place, the idea of 'criterion', as used in this issue of *Concilium*, is philosophical and basically scientific. Can it be used as a theological category? Does an irrefutable criterion of authenticity necessarily imply a reduction? Jean Ladrière's article aims to help us to approach this question by going further than the question itself and throwing light on the entire sector of epistemology. In constructing a concept of the 'human' factor, we are engaging in a secondary hermeneutical exercise with regard to effective existence, an exercise in which we ought to take account both of the historical aspect and, in theology, of the distinction between what is structural and what merely describes events.

It also seemed desirable to give some attention to the other option, in order to avoid returning to it again and again in different contexts. This option consists of a denial of the 'human' factor, either in the name of the divine element or by stressing sin and the need for flight from the world. Even a 'spiritual' humanism appears nowadays to deny certain aspects of humanity.

Antoine Vergote, who is both a psychoanalyst and a theologian, has attempted, in his article, to analyse some of the forms of what he calls a Christian 'misunderstanding' of the human element. This amounts, in his opinion, to a 'supernaturalism' in thinking, the spiritual life, the practice of the sacraments and sexual morality. Christians, he believes, have tended to wage war against pleasure and this is the most serious denial of humanity, especially in the form of incomprehensible laws of ecclesiastical authority.

In the second and essential part of this issue of *Concilium*, we have encouraged contributors to develop the complexity of the problem as fully as possible. In a fundamental article, E. Schillebeeckx has examined the status of the humen element in Christianity. Three other authors have developed, as examples, certain specific modalities. D. Mieth has considered ethics, and argues that an acceptance of the autonomy of ethics removes any possibility of our remaining neutral to the demands of ethics. N. Greinacher has reviewed the Christian's rights in the Church and their relationship with the rights of man generally in society. The third author, X. Thévenot, has given his attention to the need to overcome Christian animosity with regard to sexuality without overestimating it or making it too easy. These articles overlap to a considerable degree and their individual differences are due more to the contrasting sectors studied by the authors than to the latter's personal tendencies.

We have learnt, in approaching this question, not to contrast terms, so that there is no need to attempt to reconcile them again later. The object of our reflection in faith is the human factor. It is the integrity of this human factor that gives historical reality to the Christian element, without resulting in a confusion between the two, since the latter enables the former to become the locus where the absolute can be found. The ways in which God creates and reveals himself cannot be foreseen. This enables us to hope for the fulfilment of the human element, but we can only speak of this in metaphors or by questioning ourselves in confrontation with the suffering of our fellow-men. The Christian ethics of love do not, in the same way, contradict the autonomy of morality. The Sermon on the Mount is not neutral—it is not an ethical discourse, but an example of orthopraxis in faith, which of necessity contains a hope and has to prove its value in ethical behaviour. This conduct is not prescribed by Christian orthopraxis, but its ultimate meaning can be understood in the light of that orthopraxis.

As far as the rights of man are concerned, God appears in the Bible as the guarantor of their existence and Jesus certainly made it possible for us to have a radical understanding of the dignity of every man. This has resulted in a history which is ambiguous in two ways and in which the message of freedom is confused with the opposite message and the struggle for the rights of man has been conducted in opposition to the churches. Nonetheless, there is considerable overlapping between the rights of man in general and the Christian's rights, since everything that is human is also Christian, even if there are certain specific Christian rights within the Church. Finally, as far as sexuality is concerned, what has become fully human in the eyes of contemporary men and women is, in principle at least, in conformity with the message of the Bible. This is certainly true if we really go back to the Bible and accept that we do not need to endorse everything that has taken place at a given moment in history. The message does not, in other words, contain any higher norms, but it can point to certain impasses.

In the third part of this issue, we found that we had to return to our original plan and review it critically, if we were to avoid the temptation to construct a system and to do justice to opposing themes, so long as they formed part of the essential Christian heritage. Seen from the purely anthropological point of view, ought the 'human' factor not to be regarded as a category that is not closed in on itself, but is open to the 'divine' element? On the basis of two examples, the axiom *gratia praesupponit naturam* (Thomas Aquinas) and Karl Rahner's transcendental theology, B. Quelquejeu shows in his article that the Christian tradition has been able to satisfy the intention of a 'humanist' Christianity—salvation is the presupposition for human integrity and is adapted to it—while at the same time emphasising finite man's radical and paradoxical capacity to be open to transcendence. Quelquejeu points out, however, that this individual transcendental perspective has certain limits in the social arena within which the human interpretation of the gospel has to take place. Quelquejeu's article also points clearly to one of the aspects of the approach described *a priori* by J. Ladrière.

Following on this, we asked C. Duquoc the following question: How can certain 'ruptures', such as the foolishness of the cross, the value of apparent failure or the choice of the weak to confound the strong, have a place within the framework of a 'humanist' Christianity? As the image of the necessary renunciation of all growth and of the positive integration of the negative into our approach to God, the cross is not in itself opposed to the human factor. It is possible for it to become 'inhuman', however, in the use that is made of it and in the abstract process by which it has been universally applied. As an event, the cross points to the ambiguity of the image and is only made clear in the light of Jesus' life and his struggle for justice and against violence and oppression, which resulted in his death.

We are therefore once again brought back to that aspect with which J. Comblin deals explicitly in conclusion. This is that it is possible to approach the human factor not simply as a construction in itself, but rather as the service of one's fellow-men or as freedom that is found in giving oneself for others. This generous and firm approach avoids the ambiguities that are several times stressed in this issue of *Concilium*. These include individualism, the spread of bourgeois attitudes, the failure to recognise the wretchedness of so many men and a comforting and alienating form of colonialism. It is an approach that may succeed better than any other in drawing on the wealth contained in the theme that we have been bold enough to attack frontally—that of the authenticity of the human element as the touchstone for keeping to the Gospel message and as the way into a deeper understanding of that message.

CLAUDE GEFFRÉ
JEAN-PIERRE JOSSUA

Translated by David Smith

Peter Eicher

The Consequences of God's Humanity for the Problem of Christian Humanism

'. . . the executioners of today, as everyone knows, are humanists. Hence we cannot be too wary of the humanitarian ideology . . .'

Albert Camus[1]

1. AN ALL TOO HUMAN QUESTION?

THE DEMAND for humanity presupposes inhuman conditions. And the call for a new humanism of today arises from disillusion with the old humanisms of yesterday that have not delivered what they promised. Did not the classical humanism that the commercial bourgeoisie of Europe took with it as its better self in the luggage of colonial acquisition rob defeated civilisations of their own humanity without showing them the humanity it promised? And today, in order to safeguard the alleged humanity of the liberal free market and of socialist workers' states, has not once again a potential of destruction been built up that does not merely mock any claims to humanity but in fact threatens to extinguish mankind as a whole? And what has this ghastly rivalry between liberal-democratic and Marxist-Leninist humanisms got to offer the two thirds of mankind who live in what is termed the Third World? Is it not in fact a question of mankind as a whole, mankind as a unity, and thus of the basic humanity of every inhabitant of this earth? Have not the goods and resources of this earth run short for everyone, is it not the economic system of every country that is threatened and the vision of the future of everyone that is in danger? The question of what is worthy of man has become the basic question of what is essential to mankind. The national, cultural, class or ideological limitations of all historically transmitted humanisms have therefore been broken open by the search for a way of embodying in practice a humanity that would first of all serve the bare survival of a rapidly growing human race and then its peaceful flourishing. If in the period of development that followed the Second World War the industrial nations that were continually growing wealthier still condescendingly saw the problem of humanity as a problem for the underdeveloped countries, this just demonstrated their own underdevelopment in terms of human dignity. The economic,

1

military and social problems that were swept out of doors have now come home to roost and increase the fears at the centre of world trade: the irresistible rise in unemployment deprives the underprivileged of their self-esteem, the quarrelsomeness of the military blocs weakens political stability, and the limits that have been discerned to an economy of growth have withdrawn from industrialised humanism the basis for the benevolence it lays claim to.

Is salvation to be expected from yet another new humanism in mankind's growing crisis? Or, as was the case just before and after the Second World War, should the promised solution be called a 'Christian humanism'? Questions like this smack of ideology. It is in the name of isms like humanism, socialism and capitalism that the great battles of our history have been fought, but does Christian faith become more liberating and more redeeming today if in making its own claim it now depends on one of these isms? Faced with a threatened future, is the unique name of Jesus Christ no longer solid enough for the Christian churches, is its traditional message no longer able to make its own way in face of the new crisis, must it chum up with the great noun 'humanism' as the tiny adjective 'Christian' in order to be helpful and at last become true? It is enough to recall Jean-Jacques Rousseau's black humour to shrink back from the absurdity of looking for a 'new Christian humanism': 'We are told that a people of true Christians would form the most perfect society imaginable. I see in this supposition only one great difficulty: that a society of true Christians would not be a society of men.'[2]

Clearly it is not given to Christians to bear witness to God's basic humanity in Jesus Christ in such a way that this faith would be able to incite them and their societies to lead a life more in keeping with human dignity. Rather, Christians today are strangely enough asking themselves whether and to what extent their faith is human and whether and to what extent it is useful in the face of the great crises mankind is encountering. The international range of the questions facing mankind today thus forces us, in advance of any attempt to claim humanism for Christianity, to consider historically what the originally European concept of humanism means and the ends to which it has been applied up till the present.

2. THE DIGNITY OF HUMANISM

Recounting the history of European humanisms would mean tracing the development of the modern world in one of its most continuous forms of expression from the fourteenth century onwards.[3] However justified it may be to divide European history up into periods such as the Renaissance, the Baroque, the Enlightenment, the age of revolution and restoration, the age of imperialism and of world war, each of these periods had its own humanism. Although it would be foolish to reduce the humanist continuity of the fragmented history of the modern world to an abstract denominator, nevertheless a single intention seems to mark all the expressions of modern humanism: the unconditional aim of self-realisation, of human freedom, of defining oneself, the will to gain self-determination. In keeping with the concept of self-realisation the self certainly takes on a wide variety of forms of expression in each historical context, and what is termed freedom in contrast to actual examples of lack of freedom differs continually, but it is always here in principle that humanism derives the right to continual revolutionary self-determination. The continuity of this humanist self-determination can be shown by three examples from three historical situations that are hardly comparable: the Florentine academy at the end of the fifteenth century, the post-revolutionary idealism at the end of the eighteenth century, and the post-war existentialist humanism of the twentieth century.

(a) First Example: Fifteenth Century Florentine Thought

It is not simply by accident that the first passage dates from 1492, the year recent historiography dates the modern age from: the year when Islam was finally forced back into North Africa, when the Spaniards and Portuguese discovered the new world (Columbus), when at the same time the unrestrained persecution of the Jews was unleashed, when in Nuremberg Behaim constructed the first globe, when Leonardo da Vinci sketched his flying machine, when Copernicus began his studies in Cracow, when Lorenzo de' Medici, the great promoter of the civilisation of the Renaissance, was buried in Florence, when Alexander VI became Pope. (A year later he divided the entire new world between Spain and Portugal.) In this year, which brought together the revolutionary changes of an entire epoch, the young Giovanni Pico della Mirandola distilled the legacy of early Florentine humanism in a work that became the programme of humanism not just in Italy but in England (Thomas More), France (Guillaume Budé, Jacques Lefèvre d'Étaples), and Germany (Johannes Reuchlin, Erasmus). The title of the work expresses this programme: *De hominis dignitate,* the dignity of man.[4] Man's dignity still depends on God's word; but the freedom God creates consists precisely in man's ability to free himself from this origin. Once the supreme architect of the world had fully constructed his creation, nothing more remained than to form a man from it. According to Pico della Mirandola God thus gave man as his possession everything that already existed:

'Therefore he accepted man as a creature with no clear distinguishing features and, placing him in the middle of the world, told him: "We have not given you any definite habitation, Adam, or face of your own, or any gift unique to you, so that you may have and possess as you wish and think fit whichever habitation, whichever face, whichever gift you desire. The other beings have a fixed nature that is bound by laws we have prescribed. You are bound by no limitations and will exercise your judgment, to which we have entrusted you, in defining your nature for yourself. I have placed you in the middle of the world . . . We have made you neither of heaven nor of earth, neither mortal nor immortal, so that you may freely and honourably use your judgment in shaping and fashioning yourself into whichever form you prefer".'[5]

Pico's aim, as a pupil of the Christian Platonist Marsilio Ficino and drawing on all the rhetoric of a universalist education that extended from Iranian Zoroastrianism by way of Orphic mysticism, gnosticism and the Fathers of the Church to Islamic mysticism and the Jewish cabbala, was to establish a spiritualist ethics of the rise of the soul to divinity. What cannot be ignored is the break with the scholastic incorporation of man in the hierarchical order of creation. It is here, and not in the theology of Albertus Magnus and Thomas Aquinas, that man becomes dependent on himself, that anthropocentricity finds its modern expression, that theology is based on human freedom and no longer on God's creative providence. The new language and style correspond to the new self-awareness of a primitive bourgeoisie that was everywhere breaking through the narrow limitations of the old feudal system as shown by the commercial trade and the money economy of European cities from the thirteenth century onwards.[6] It is futile to use the term humanism for every expression of culture in which man makes himself the subject, because in that case right from the Bible and Homer via scholasticism up to the ecological movement today everything is blurred by the ideological incense of the human factor and can be justified ideologically. The term humanism, first coined at the start of the nineteenth century,[7] has as its object that programme of cultural education we owe to the humanists of the Renaissance: they shifted the emphasis in education away from metaphysics, from logic, from mathematics, from Roman law and from scholastic theology to classical literature. The *studia humanitatis* of grammar, rhetoric, history, poetry and ethics would now open up the alternative world of Greece and Rome to put paid to the new outdated world of scholasticism and feudal law ('renaissance').[8] True, the aim was not yet to develop an anti-Christian universe, but still it was to use all the available resources of language to strengthen and celebrate 'confidence in the value of man' (Kristeller).[9] A humanist image of man therefore only exists to the extent that man develops his own image of himself and lives on the basis of this—whether he aims to develop himself in a 'Christian', a 'liberal-revolutionary' or a 'socialist' sense. In the understanding of the dignity of freedom that is proper to it, humanist mankind corresponds not to just any history at all but to the history of the European bourgeoisie in its revolutionary character from the fourteenth century on: as the passage quoted from Pico della Mirandola shows, the humanists burst the bonds of natural relationships in order to justify their new world by referring back to the universalist aspects of the world of Greece and Rome. But this new world began to exert colonial sway beyond the narrow confines of the feudal system and the city states, it began to keep a statistical account of its own relationships, as Jacob Burckhardt stressed a long time ago,[10] and in doing so to value individuals, and equally the attractiveness of a free and sophisticated social life became prominent, as did awareness of the landscape within which man was placed. Everywhere the sphinx, who knows all riddles, answered man's urgent questions with the single response: 'You are the solution to the riddle—you, man, 'The world is your world', 'It is your creation'. The arts—architecture, sculpture and painting—became the language of man transforming everything in his own image.

(b) Second Example: Eighteenth Century Post-revolutionary Idealism

While the classical humanism of the fourteenth to sixteenth centuries referred back to the classical world in order to shape its present, the idealistic humanism of the period after the French Revolution looked to its own awareness of freedom in order to shape the future. The tradition of the classical world and Christianity was as such done away with and only still applied when it could be brought to the level of the prevailing idea of freedom. A second passage will make this clear.

In Germany, where the revolutions of history take place only belatedly and then only inside people's heads, Johann Gottlieb Fichte provided a systematic exposition of the humanist ideal of education in the sense of the revolutionary awareness of freedom. 'Now it is time to make the people acquainted with the freedom it will find as soon as it is aware of it,' he wrote. '. . . Now is the moment of the dawn beginning to break, and full daylight will follow in its time.[11] But freedom is something people can only be aware of if it is expected of everyone and if everyone wants to make use of it. Here it is no longer a question of a creator God ascribing freedom to man from outside, but of the will to freedom that historically has broken through in the revolution demanding as it were of itself to re-work all relationships in a spirit of freedom:

'The source of all my . . . thoughts and even of my life itself—that from which everything proceeds which can have an existence in me, for me, or through me, the innermost spirit of my spirit—is no longer a foreign power; it is, in the strictest possible sense, my own reasonable act. I am wholly my own creation. I might have followed blindly the leading of my spiritual nature, but I resolve to be a work not of Nature but of myself, and I have become so even by means of this resolution.'[12]

Anyone who accepts freedom in this way will at the same time be aware of his or her responsibility for everybody's freedom, since freedom appears not as something that is already there but as something that ought to belong to all relationships. The requirement of conscience demands the recognition of every other freedom and contains 'the absolute demand for a better world',[13] in other words a political and economic order based on freedom, an educational system and a religion of freedom that subsumes the earthly kingdom in that of eternity. But as we have pointed out Fichte's revolution takes place in people's heads, in education, and thus remains within the framework of classical humanism. When it finds actual expression it aims on the one hand at a mystical inwardness in which God creates the image of his absolute freedom in human consciousness, and on the other hand externally at an unrestrained educational dictatorship directed at freedom and nationalist self-assertion. In its historical inwardness and in its external arrogance Fichte's humanism displays the basic traits of bourgeois religion,[14] of religious humanism transcending all denominations. One aspect of it is that it liberates the 'savage tribes', as Fichte calls them, of the non-European world from their crude sensuousness and cultivates them: 'They will thereby be brought into union with the great whole of humanity and be made capable of taking part in its further progress'—even if this is by means of 'natural wars' with 'uncivilized peoples'.[15] Thanks to the higher humanity of the Germans liberated by education it 'must be that they are the victors . . . and so the entire human race on earth will be embraced by a unique inwardly allied Christian state which can now follow a joint plan of the conquest of nature and then enter the higher sphere of another life'.[16] This universal reign of terror also belongs to the consequences of Europeans' humanist desire for freedom.

(c) Third Example: Twentieth Century Post-War Existentialist Humanism

The well-informed reader will be aware of what must now ensue, for there is in fact a direct line from Pico della Mirandola's classical humanism to Fichte's revolutionary humanism and then on to the existential humanism of Jean-Paul Sartre. After the catastrophic destruction of the bourgeois world in the Second World War, any restoration of a world of Christian western education and culture along Renaissance lines had become impossible, as had any idealistic accomplishment of revolutionary freedom. It thus became a question of settling accounts with the forms of classical humanism. The humanism that set man up as its goal and took him as a higher value had shown itself to be a *reductio ad absurdum:* 'The cult of humanity ends in Comtian humanism, shut-in upon itself, and—this must be said—in Fascism. We do not want a humanism like that.[17] Hence Sartre's critical humanism tries to think through consistently to its logical conclusion what it means if man becomes man neither through some pre-ordained creation or nature nor through the supposed laws of history and its goal. Thus he talks of another meaning of humanism:

'Man is all the time outside of himself: it is in projecting and losing himself beyond himself that he makes man to exist; and, on the other hand, it is by pursuing transcendent aims that he himself is able to exist. Since man is thus self-surpassing, he is himself the heart and centre of his transcendence. There is no other universe except the human universe, the universe of human subjectivity. . . . it is this that we call existential humanism. This is humanism, because we remind man that there is no legislator but himself; . . .

'Existentialism is nothing else but an attempt to draw the full conclusions from a consistently atheistic position . . . even if God existed that would make no difference from its point of view.'[18]

True, this passage which once stimulated an entire generation now reads rather flatly because it is unable to provide orientation either for the revolution of 1968 or for the movements of liberation in the third world or for the ecological alternatives to be found within the peace movement today. This is because it is not able to link awareness of freedom with becoming aware of those necessary changes of structure that are able to make freedom an actual reality. More profoundly, when man may never be man because it is still something he has to become, he remains inhuman, he cannot be what he ought to be. Sartre's revolutionary rigorism, which deprives man of that innate dignity to bestow on him the freedom of continual transcendence, does not only remain absurd (which is indeed its intention) but becomes a terror of self-realisation without the consolation of grace. Although Sartre's analysis merely repeats superficially and in psychological language what Fichte had already put forward, the consequences remain the same: the imposition of decisions in practice corresponds to a rigorous concentration on inward realities. To this the necessary objections have long since been raised by the Reformers, criticism of classical humanism and Marx's of idealistic humanism.

3. THE PROTEST

We must emphasise once again that for a long time it has been impossible completely to define or even to explain the humanist movement with its wealth of expression by referring to some root determinant cause, even if this is that of autonomous humanity. But theology needs to know what terrain it is operating on if today it wishes to become humanist once again. The history of modern Christianity is full of theologies that have conformed to the humanisms of the moment—and equally full of energetic theological protests against this kind of procedure. The confrontation always centres on the single point of the problem of freedom and servitude, of master and servant. Can man become master of himself, lord of nature and the shaper of the social and political order to make freedom a reality, or by this attempt at self-realisation does he merely involve himself more deeply in dependence with regard to his will to power? Is man able to develop himself and his situation freely, or is he always so entangled in the relationships that dominate him that he cannot attain to freedom under his own steam? To put it in theological terms, is man capable of himself willing and gaining his own salvation, or is he dominated by sin to such an extent that all his attempts to liberate himself merely drive him more deeply into despair? Does he need redemption, does he need grace, in order to become a free human being? Does history need God's creative domination to become a realm of freedom—or can it when given a humanist shape itself become a history of salvation?

Against the princes of Christian humanism, against Erasmus, Martin Luther brought into play the fact of the enslavement of all human struggles for freedom, which remained an expression of selfishness. In the light of the liberating act of redemption in which God sacrifices himself, to the point of accepting the cross, to the consequences of human self-realisation in order to take its curse on himself, the ethical optimism of the humanists appears as foolish self-delusion and as the height of ingratitude for God's gracious act of reconciliation. Blaise Pascal similarly mocked Montaigne's humanist cult of personality: 'He encourages an indifference towards salvation'[19]— as well as the bourgeois religion of the Jesuits, 'who even go so far as to assert that the advantage Jesus Christ brought the world consisted of being able to renounce loving God',[20] since man liberated for freedom could now attain salvation by his own moral efforts without God's love. Should we go on to recall Calvin's glorification of God's election of grace as against Zwingli's efforts in a humanist direction, Kierkegaard's dialectic of despair as against Hegel's attempt to claim the history of mankind as the history of freedom? Or is it enough to point out that in the course of this criticism Marx exposed classical humanism as the necessary ideology of a bourgeoisie that had became incapable of humanising actual existing relationships? Clearly the history of the criticism of humanism teaches us not only about what remains unredeemed in the various forms of humanism but also about the fact that criticism does not solve the fundamental humanist problem. Nor is any solution possible as long as one continues to recognise that every human project is not the plaything of chance and necessity but stands within the responsibility of freedom, however this may be interpreted. Thus for the young Marx Communism itself becomes 'perfect humanism' and transcends the classical humanism he is criticising to become 'the *genuine* resolution of the conflict between man and nature and between man and man—the true resolution of the strife . . . between freedom and necessity, between the individual and the species. Communism is the riddle of history solved, and it knows itself to be this solution.[21] But clearly this solved riddle has not settled the conflict once and for all but has increased its potential with regard to the political claims it can make. The root of the battle of humanism that flares up again in Marxism itself must lie in the fact that the fundamental bourgeois problem of unrestrained domination over nature and freedom can never be resolved in the Marxist programme of self-realisation through work.[22] Even the Catholic theologians who, like Jacques Maritain, called for the 'secular or profane Christianity' of the 'new, integral humanism' as against 'liberal bourgeois humanism' when faced with growing catastrophe in the 1930s[23] ultimately failed in their doomed attempt to save the modern world by means of a past civilisation. The tragedy of bourgeois humanism could no longer be transcended by the efforts at conjuration of a West that before the war had in vain been disinterred as a Christian humanist entity.

If in 1945 in the still smoking rubble of the bombed cities Hugo Rahner solemnly declared that Christians now 'know that God's eternal word has deigned to descend to this area of western civilisation in order from there to draw to itself the minds of the whole earth and to bring them home to the wonderful community of a Christian humanism,[24] we know today that salvation has not come from the West and its humanism. Does the idea of Christian humanism therefore remain merely a dream, an ideology of an intellectual élite, the failed attempt of an abstract desire for freedom that continually ends in historical terror? Or must not Christian faith give an account of how it defines what is human and where in its view mankind is going?

4. REDEMPTION TO BECOME HUMAN

The Gospel of the Old and New Testament recognises neither a humanism nor a theism: the contrast between these two is something quite unknown to it. The Gospel does not make man great in his power to create civilisation but in the fact that his sins have been forgiven, that he has been redeemed from his inhumanity and brought out of slavery. The Gospel does not speak of the almighty in the metaphysical language of domination but bears witness to the word of God that is powerful in the powerlessness of history, strong in the weakness of the cross, victorious in death. There is no more human language to talk of man and his world than that of the Old and New Gospel: according to this witness, the world of man has been created in the word that became man on the cross of history: 'in whom we have redemption, the forgiveness of sins . . . for in him all things were created, in heaven and on earth, visible and invisible, whether thrones or dominions or principalities or authorities' (Col. 1:14, 16).

The Christian confession of faith is not supported by an idea of God nor based on an idea of man, however lofty that may be, but rather lives on the basis of thanking God for what he has done to Israel and through Israel's son Jesus Christ to all men and women. The Christian doctrine of man is thus an acknowledgement of God's redeeming action, in the same way as the Christian doctrine of the nature of the universe and of man is an acknowledgement of his creative action. And this acknowledgement does not celebrate abstract concepts about God's humanity or man's divinity but bears actual witness to God's own eternal word that became man in this one man out of the whole multitude of men, Jesus of Nazareth: no humanist, no religious hero, but a poor, rejected, condemned man. The majesty of God is to be found in the humbled humanity of his son: the humanity of man is to be found in being taken up in redemption into this divine sonship. It is here that one can talk of 'God's humanism'[25] as Karl Barth did in the retractation in which in masterly fashion he overcame his original resentment against every kind of humanist way of being a Christian: 'No, God requires no exclusion of humanity, no non-humanity, not to speak of inhumanity, in order to be truly God.'[26]

B

If therefore we can in this sense talk of the humanist confession of the Christian faith,[27] then the only criterion for what is human remains the actual humanity of Jesus Christ and not the abstract freedom of human nature.

What does this mean?

First of all it means simply the recognition of the unheard-of novelty of the Gospel, that God himself wants to belong to mankind and has eternally linked himself to it. God wanted to be as human in himself, in his own word, as in Jesus of Nazareth he has become for all men. To speak in humanist terms, Christians allow their freedom to be completely determined by the free act of God's creative, elective and redeeming action, they allow themselves to be defined by the history of God's dealings with mankind. From this follows secondly the passionate interest of Christians in all human, humanitarian and humanist movements of liberation which themselves bear the traits of God's merciful, loyal and just humanity. Hence Christians must on the other hand let themselves be recalled to their humanity, to the humanity of Jesus Christ, by the inexorable criticism of the Church and of ideology mounted by the modern idea of freedom. What cannot be overlooked is the way the Christian churches have distorted and concealed the human face of God and the way this face has appeared in countless movements and among countless individuals who have left the Christian churches and fought against them on account of their lack of humanity. Hence it is necessary to stress the adjective 'human' today before the noun 'Jesus Christ' and if necessary to promote a human and humane Christianity in this sense.[28]

The consequence of God's humanity is therefore not to be found in a new humanist ethics for mankind but in the fact that on this age of ours, as on the age preceding it and that which will follow, God's merciful, just and faithful grace has been bestowed so that it can become human:

Because he is our peace and has made peace (Eph. 2:14-16) we are happy that we have to make peace (Matt. 5:9)—against all the crazy security measures arming us for death.

Because everything has been created in him, we are happy that we do not have to dominate nature but must enable nature to share in the redeemed freedom of the children of God (Rom. 5:21).

Because he liberates his people we are happy if we hunger and thirst for justice and are persecuted for its sake (Matt. 5:6, 10).

Because he goes as far as the cross in his humanity, we must be human for other people to the point of our own breakdown.

Because he has reconciled the world to himself, we who are Godless must live and die in his peace.

The way of the Gospel does not divide us from those who exchange their lives for others in the name of freedom and justice. It enables us to go along with them. Perhaps it is only the hope that we can remain human for ever that distinguishes us from those who as humanists despair of themselves and their world.

Translated by Robert Nowell

Notes

1. Albert Camus 'Reflections on the Guillotine' in *Resistance, Rebellion and Death* (London 1961) p. 163.

2. Jean-Jacques Rousseau *The Social Contract and Discourses*, translated with an introduction by G. D. H. Cole (London/New York 1913) p. 111 (book IV, chapter 8).

3. Of fundamental importance remain Jacob Burckhardt *The Civilization of the Renaissance in Italy* (London 1965); Wilhelm Dilthey *Weltanschauung und Analyse des Menschen seit Renaissance und Reformation* (collected works vol. II) (Stuttgart/Göttingen 1969); Paul Oskar Kristeller

Renaissance Thought. The classic, scholastic and humanist strains (New York 1961); *Renaissance Thought. II Papers on humanism and the arts* (New York 1965); R. Weimann, W. Lenk, and J. J. Slomka *Renaissanceliteratur und frühbürgerliche Revolution* (Berlin/Weimar 1976).

4. Giovanni Pico della Mirandola *de Hominis Dignitate, Heptaplus, de Ente et Uno,* etc., edited by Eugenio Gazin (Florence 1942).

5. *Ibid.* pp. 104-106.

6. See R. Weimann, the work cited in note 3, p. 13. For the differentiation of the relationship between spiritual universality and abstract monetary value see R. W. Müller, *Geld und Geist. Zur Entstehungsgeschichte von Identitätsbewusstsein und Rationalität seit der Antike* (Frankfurt/New York 1977).

7. The term was introduced in 1808 by the German educationalist F. J. Niethammer: see the entry by R. Romberg s.v. *Humanismus, Humanität,* in *Historisches Wörterbuch der Philosophie* III col. 1217. The first instance cited by the Oxford English Dictionary dates from 1812, when Coleridge used it in the obsolete sense of belief in the mere humanity of Christ: the earliest examples in its other current senses date from the 1830s.

8. See Paul Oskar Kristeller, in the work cited in note 3, vol. I, pp. 15-20; Johan Huizinga *Das Problem der Renaissance Renaissance und Realismus* (Darmstadt 1974).

9. Paul Oskar Kristeller, the work cited in note 3, vol. I, p. 28.

10. See Jacob Burckhardt, the work cited in note 3, pp. 50-52.

11. Johann Gottlieb Fichte *Beitrag zur Berechtigung des Publicums über die französische Revolution,* Works, ed. I. H. Fichte (Berlin 1971) vol. VI, p. 45.

12. Johann Gottlieb Fichte *The Vocation of Man* (New York 1956) p. 91.

13. *Ibid.* p. 100.

14. See D. Schellong *Bürgertum und christliche Religion* (Munich 1975) pp. 7-28; Peter Eicher 'Von den Schwierigkeiten bürgerlicher Theologie mit den katholischen Kirchenstrukturen' in Heinrich Fries and Karl Rahner *Theologie in Freiheit und Verantwortung* (Munich 1981) pp. 96-137, with further literature cited there.

15. Johann Gottlieb Fichte *The Vocation of Man* p. 106.

16. Johann Gottlieb Fichte *Die Staatslehre* (1813), Works, vol. IV, p. 600.

17. Jean-Paul Sartre *Existentialism and Humanism* (London 1948) p. 55.

18. *Ibid.* pp. 55-56.

19. Blaise Pascal *Pensées* (936 Lafuma, 63 Brunschvig, 77 Chevalier), translated with an introduction by Martin Turnell, London, 1962, p. 410.

20. Blaise Pascal *Les Provinciales,* in *Oeuvres complètes,* ed. J. Chevalier (Paris 1954) p. 778; see also Bernard Groethuysen *The Bourgeois: Catholicism vs. Capitalism in eighteenth century France* (London 1968).

21. See Karl Marx *Economic and Philosophic Manuscripts of 1844* in Karl Marx and Friedrich Engels *Collected Works,* (London 1975) III, pp. 296-297.

22. Karl Marx *Kritik des Gothaer Programms* in Karl Marx and Friedrich Engels, *Werke* (Berlin 1962) XIX, pp. 15 ff.

23. Jacques Maritain *True Humanism* (London 1938) p. xvi.

24. Hugo Rahner *Abendland. Reden und Aufsätze* (Freiburg/Basle 1966) p. 15.

25. Karl Barth *Humanismus* (Zürich 1950) p. 4.

26. Karl Barth *The Humanity of God* (London 1961, 1967) p. 47.

27. On this see Rudolf Bultmann's efforts at mediation in 'Humanismus und Christentum' in his *Glauben und Verstehen,* (Tübingen 1952) II, pp. 133-148, where he attempts a pragmatic reconciliation of the historical dialectic between biblical faith and modern humanisms.

28. For the necessary dialectic between the modern idea of freedom and the Gospel proclaimed by the Church, see Peter Eicher 'Von den Schwierigkeiten bürgerlicher Theologie mit den katholischen Kirchenstrukturen, in Heinrich Fries and Karl Rahner *Theologie in Freiheit und Verantwortung* (Munich 1981) pp. 96-137, and Peter Eicher *Theologie. Eine Einführung in das Studium* (Munich 1980) pp. 211-230.

Jean Ladrière

On the Notion of Criterion

THE CONTEXTS in which the notion of criterion is used are varied, but there is perhaps one area in which this notion has a particularly clear part to play and which might constitute a paradigmatic context: the area of epistemology. The concept of criterion is involved in relation to two questions of capital importance: that of scientific status and that of validity.

The *question of scientific status* was posed in a radical way be neo-positivism in its early days, in the form of the problem of meaning. According to the presuppositions of empiricism, only those propositions which can be interpreted in the final analysis in terms of perceptual data are endowed with meaning. As the domain of scientific propositions (and of those which may be considered as capable of being assimilated to them, which is true in the case of many propositions of ordinary speech) is considered to coincide exactly with the domain of propositions endowed with meaning, the problem of the criterion of meaning and that of the criterion of scientific status are identical. Criticising the sweeping statements of neo-positivism, Popper has modified the terms of the question and has posed the problem of scientific status in the form of a problem of demarcation. What is at issue, in his version, is not the determining of the necessary and sufficient conditions whereby a given proposition may be considered to be endowed with meaning, but the determining of the necessary and sufficient conditions for considering a given proposition to belong to the domain of science (inasmuch as the latter may be separated in this way from other domains, such as that of metaphysics, which are not, for all that, dismissed as having no meaning). The answer to the question posed in these terms is given by the criterion of falsifiability.

What matters to us here is not the examination of the pertinence of this criterion, and its possible superiority when compared with others, but the way in which a criterion of demarcation may be established. One simple method would consist in starting from an *a priori* idea of science, either discovered in a field of evidence which is already open to intellectual investigation or else elaborated on the basis of a process of philosophical reflection on the conditions of knowledge in the form of concepts. It would then be enough to attempt to explicate, in terms of necessary and sufficient conditions, the content of that idea. But we are compelled to recognise that we do not have at our disposal an apriorism of that kind. One may indeed recall to mind the old idea of a 'knowledge according to principles' but that would not be comprehensive enough to indicate precisely the way in which a science like physics differs from metaphysics. In reality, every discussion relating to the criterion of demarcation takes as its starting point a science which is already established, and clearly takes as its frame of reference that scientific discipline which appears to us today to be the most perfect realisation of an empirical type of knowledge and which therefore seems to us to deserve in the highest degree the predicate 'scientific' (in the contemporary sense of that term), i.e. physics. (This discussion is not concerned with the purely formal sciences.) This means that the real guiding principle of this quest is not an idea but a practical system which is already established, considered in its historical evolution. It can thus be seen that the epistemological process which seeks to formulate an adequate criterion of demarcation is itself controlled by a secondary criterion which determines the condition of adequacy of the criterion which is being sought: the latter must be of such a kind that it must, in every case, be valid for the propositions of physics and it must, on the other hand, not be valid in every case for the propositions of metaphysics. It might be possible to show that disciplines other than physics satisfy this criterion and one could possibly also attempt to pronounce, on the basis of this criterion, on the status of practices whose scientific character is a matter of controversy (such as psychoanalysis). But in any event one would be proceeding on the basis of a case which is judged to be perfectly clear-cut.

Now if physics is recognised as having this privileged status, this is not because it has been elaborated in conformity with certain pre-existing criteria (possibly of another type) but because it has revealed in its historical development, and relying on its own resources, a remarkable type of epistemic activity, ensuring the possibility of an agreement which is in principle universal and the possibility of progress which is in principle unlimited. The search for a criterion is, then, in the final analysis, merely an attempt to make explicit an immanent normative quality which had developed within physics progressively, at the same time as physics itself was becoming constituted. One cannot, it seems, account for its becoming formed in this way merely in terms of an 'international aim' or a 'theological interest', nor, consequently, can one locate the norm within the internal dynamism of the knowing subject. One must conclude, rather, that the latter merely becomes progressively aware, during the actual functioning of the operative system which he is constructing, of conditions of efficacity which the progress of construction itself renders both increasingly precise and increasingly compelling.

The examination of the *question of validity* would give rise to similar considerations. When one attempts to determine on what conditions a scientific proposition may be considered to be valid, and what degree of validity may be accorded to it, one does not rely on an *a priori* idea of validity but on the practical procedures by means of which the recognised scientific disciplines estimate the value of the propositions which they construct. Thus, the search for a criterion of validity is itself guided, exactly as in the case of the criterion of scientific status, by a secondary criterion: the criterion being sought must be of such a kind that it may in every case be valid for the propositons which are in fact accepted in the scientific discipline which may be considered to be paradigmatic and that it may not be valid for the propositions which are rejected by that discipline. As for the procedures for acceptance and rejection, they are constituted, not under the control of pre-existing rules, but in an immanent way, within the actual process of the constitution of the disciplines of which they form a part. These conclusions may be enlightening where the possible introduction of the notion of criterion in theology is concerned. If one may consider the case of epistemology as paradigmatic, it must be recognised that (1) a criterion cannot function as an *a priori* determinant but only as a retrospective expression of an immanent normative quality, and (2) the formulation of a directly operative criterion must be regulated by a secondary criterion which, in fact, refers back to the process whereby that immanent normative quality is constituted. The question posed here amounts to asking whether, and on what conditions, the human can constitute a theological criterion. This question immediately divides into two: it is first necessary to ask whether there exists a concept of the human, which exists prior to theology and might be invoked as a criterion—one must then ask how a possible criterion of the human might function in a theological context.

One may think of elaborating a concept of the human by starting either from an empirical basis or else from a reflective one. In the first case, one will seek to isolate observable characteristics which seem specific to the human phenomenon. But in order to be able to affirm that a given characteristic (for example the ability to make tools, or the use of language, or the cult of the dead) is specific to the human group (i.e. is found *only* within that group and is found in *every* member of that group) one must, of necessity, already have available from some other source some description of the characteristics of the human enabling one to recognise without any ambiguity the fact that a living individual belongs to the human group. To avoid an infinite regress one must necessarily rely, in the final analysis, on some non-empirical characteristic and therefore refer back to a concept which is constructed on a reflexive basis. The reflexive process of construction starts with the human phenomenon as it is given itself and seeks to discover its constitutive structures. Such a process is obviously only possible if the human being possesses in advance, by reason of his ontological structure, an understanding of himself which may make possible an explication which is conceptually structured. In fact, reflection only renders accessible in the form of language that pre-comprehension which belongs to man's being and which it recognises, moreover, as an essential moment of its own constitution. Whether the concept of the human is that of the living being endowed with speech, or that of reason-liberty, or that of openness to the transcendental, or that of self-awareness, or that of the 'shepherd of the being', it is always the recapitulation in words of a self-apprehension which is not a pure intuition but an interpretative elucidation. It is far more a question of an interpretation, of a hermeneutic type, (as may be seen in Heidegger's *Being and Time*) than of the direct reading of an essence. This means that the self-comprehension of man's being is also, of necessity, a self-evaluation, that this being only understands himself by adopting a position in relation to himself, such that the way in which he states himself to himself is an *intrinsic* part of his active manifestation and helps to determine what becomes of him.

It can thus be seen that the construction of a concept of the human, considered as a hermeneutics of existence, can only be considered as a secondary stage in relation to the actual implementation of existence, in its debate with itself, inasmuch as the latter takes place against a horizon of enlightenment which must itself be elucidated in the form of a reflective process which seeks to understand the truth about the relationship of existence to being. If this is the case, reflection must of necessity be affected by the conditions which determine constitutively the pre-comprehension of existence. In particular, it must be affected by the historical dimension which, as it shows itself, belongs to the conditions of existence. This means that the reflexive act of possession of the human by itself is not some sort of intemporal apprehension which is capable, at least in principle, of grasping adequately, in a single act, the content of man's being, but a thought-process consisting of a perpetual reassumption and reinterpretation of previously acquired data, taking place against the horizon, which is always open to change, of new possibilities of understanding. Now if there is always the possibility of a re-evaluation of reflection, this is not only because conceptualisation is always inadequate and always awaiting more appropriate reformulations, but also, and even essentially, because, in its very movement, existence reveals new forms of itself and is perpetually re-evaluating itself. When the question is looked at from this point of view it should be possible to see the place of the contribution of the 'human sciences' to the reflection process. They should be seen not as providing 'data' which reflection has merely to record or on the basis of which a more adequate concept of essence might be erected, by means of an inductive process, but as belonging to that experience which existence has of itself and thus as contributing to the reconstruction and the expansion of the pre-comprehension which reflection has the task of formulating conceptually.

Furthermore, if we wish to recognise fully the significance of the category of historicity, a dimension must be introduced into our reflection on existence between the structural order and the order of actual events. The dimensions which constitute existence, such as temporality, language, relationship to others, affectivity or action, are still merely the conditons for the possibility of its actual manifestation. In so far as they organise, as it were, in advance, independently of any particular content, the essential modalities in which existence is capable of structuring itself, they may be considered as the structural framework of existence. Historicity itself, as a dimension, is one part of that framework. But what actually takes place in the concrete processes in which a specific existence assumes its own situation and constructs its own destiny belongs to the category of events. The type of reflection in which the *possibility* of the event is conceived (inasmuch as it is set within the constructive dimensions of existence, within its structure) is entirely different from the type of reflection in which the event, as such, is recapitulated. The discourse of possibility belongs, like that of structure, to that discursive language which reproduces, in its own mode of articulation, the system of constitutive forms which is, as it were, the organising apriorism of existence. The discourse of events belongs to a language of self-implication, in and by which existence defines its position in relation to whatever affects it in the form of a provocation, call, activator, encounter, disruptive force or source of metamorphosis.

These considerations may throw some light, at least from the methodological point of view, on the question of the involvement of a possible criterion of the human in theology. They suggest in effect that this question itself depends on the following preliminary question: Should theology be considered as one stage of a reflective process relating to the constitutive structures of existence, or as a reflective process relating to an order of events which is determined (and is, perhaps, at the same time determining with regard to existence as such, considered from the viewpoint of events)? In the first case, it will have a contribution to make, as a stage in time, to the elaboration of a concept of the human, by stressing what the historical experience of Christianity provides as matter for reflection, inasmuch as it reveals certain dimensions of man's being which it alone has brought to the light of understanding. (One could show for example how the Christian experience has revealed to reflection the dimension of historicity and that of inner freedom.) And this concept, constructed (or more exactly reconstructed) in this way, could possibly become a criterion not only for theology but also for any form of reflection concerning the being and destiny of man. (Such a criterion would quite simply be the intellectual expression of an historically constituted pre-comprehension and would operate under the control of a secondary criterion, which would compel reflection to take as the guide for its own operations the historical experience of Christianity, considered as a privileged and normative area for the constitution of the pre-comprehension of existence.)

In the second case, theology, operating on the basis of an order of events which had already been historically realised, and moreover interpreting itself as a reflexive assumption of that order and as participating therefore in its character as an event, will have the task of examining itself as to its own possible nature as a discourse of events. Thus the question which it will first have to answer is whether the order of events with which it is aligned (and to which it is subordinated) should be understood as the mere occurrence of certain facts, requiring a word of ratification, recognition, celebration or thanksgiving, not a discourse of comprehension, or whether it should be understood as including within itself a structure which requires a discursive understanding, which itself forms a conceptual structure. If it is this second element of the alternative which should be retained, it will naturally be necessary to consider what, in the category of events, provides the basis for the possibility of a specific discursive treatment (of which the particular conditions determine the modality of meaning proper to theological discourse). If a discourse of the event is possible, it is, apparently, because it is produced in conformity with a certain structural order. The structure of the event is different in nature from the constructive structure of existence, which as yet only provides the conditions of possibility for the event. It might be said that the structure of the event is the system formed by the determining factors according to which it is produced and in which it finds its effective existence: this system, moreover, only has reality within the actual texture of the event.

It is the task of theology itself, of course, and not of a reflective process of a structural kind (which is only related to the event as a category) to establish its position in relation to the two questions which have just been posed. It can only do so on the basis of a certain interpretation of what constitutes the object of its discourse. This means that the understanding of theology by itself is already a theological question and that it presupposes the taking up of a position, in which the theologian puts himself in question as to his own existence, in relation to Christian experience. But how may the question of criterion be posed if theology is understood not as one stage of a reflective process of a structural kind, nor as an expression of recognition, but as a discourse of the event? If it is understood in this way, it is admitted *ipso facto* that theological discourse is related to an order of events *and* that the latter contains a specific structure. For the sake of simplicity, let us call the reflective process concerned with the constitutive structures of existence primary reflection, and the process which deals with events secondary reflection. Secondary reflection has the task not only of analysing the structure of events but also of determining how this structure is connected with that of existence. Now this connection may be conceived of in two ways: either the structures of existence, inasmuch as they merely establish conditions of possibility, are considered as being, as it were, neutral with regard to actual realisation in the sphere of events, and as invariable with regard to whatever may happen to existence in its encounter with the event, or else, in so far as they are understood in themselves simply as drafts of possible ways of being realised, they are considered as only being able to become fully determined by what happens in the events of which they are the infrastructure.

In the first case, the concept of the human elaborated in primary reflection may be taken up, unchanged, by secondary reflection, but this can only be a question of a formal concept (relative to pure forms, describing pure apriorisms), incapable of providing a criterion which could serve as a guiding principle for secondary reflection. At the very most, it might be possible, in that case, to formulate a criterion of non-contradiction: no contradiction can exist between what occurs in the sphere of events and a part of its conditons of possibility (that part which is, in fact, related to the structures of the human). But these conditions are purely formal, such a criterion must itself remain purely formal. In the second case, the concept of the human elaborated by primary reflection must be considered insufficient and as requiring a reinterpretation, in secondary reflection, in the light of what occurs in the actual event. What occurs must here be understood as having a revelatory power, not only with regard to what is presented to existence, in its actual manifestation, in its destiny, but also with regard to its constitutive structures. Doubtless what is revealed by primary reflection is already illuminating and conserves its validity even when it is subsumed into secondary reflection. A reinterpretation is not the substituion for a given reading of another reading which no longer has any connection with the first. It is a re-reading, which gives greater depth to the first, but by means, nevertheless, of a re-evaluation which causes it to be seen in a different way, against a more fully comprehensive background. The event-centred understanding of the structure, setting it in an order of realisation in which it becomes operative not as a pure form but as the supporting structure of a destiny, modifies its significance. On the basis of such an understanding, theological reflection may elaborate a criterion which will be specific to itself. Such a criterion will merely be the making explicit of the immanent normative quality which is, in fact, that of the order of events to which the reflection itself, being theological, belongs. And the construction of this criterion will be governed by a secondary criterion, according to which theology requires of itself that it should regulate its procedures in accordance with the self-comprehension of the order of events. This requirement is merely the recognition of the autonomy of that order and of the interpretation for which it provides the basis.

The fact remains nevertheless that primary reflection contains its own truth and that the order of events necessarily subsumes within itself the functioning of the structures, as this is revealed (albeit partially) in that reflection. As a result, the task of discovering how these structures are to be subsumed remains an essential one for theology.

Translated by L. H. Ginn

Antoon Vergote

Christian Misreadings of the Human

IT HAS never been the intention of Christianity to deny the human. While affirming it in theological principles, however, it has nevertheless often denied it in practice. This contradiction does not spring from desire to be perverse; it is the result of a misreading. The human has not been fully recognised, understood and esteemed even though the humanity of the human man was honoured as a sign of divine glory. This paradox results from the very essence of Christianity and the historical nature of man. The tension between the order of creation and the anticipation of eschatology in the revelation and resurrection of Jesus Christ entails an ambiguous relationship to the world. Furthermore, the believer's conviction that sin distorts human history exposes the misery which detracts from the greatness of man. The history of humanity, for its part, complicates the Christian situation even more. Man is of course not a stationary being; the subject of history, he transforms himself and wins his freedom through mastery of the determinisms of the world and of his own being. Borne along by the heady dream of realising himself totally, man opposes the message which reminds him of his divine destiny, and this conflict provokes the Church to contest the human realities thus obscured. New ideas and movements are not always totally positive, for desires and passions also feed illusions in them and prompt sacrifices to idols.

We do not deny the base actions of men of the Church that historiography keeps before us. They are a warning to us that religious hypocrisy can conceal cupidity or the will to power. But to attach too much importance to this is to misread the true problem of the realtionship between Christianity and culture. This relationship always was and always will be an unstable pact, precisely because of the ideas which Christianity introduces as well as the motive forces which work within cultures. Conflicts between Christianity and man are therefore inevitable. 'Christian humanism' will never be able to achieve a serene peace. There is no pre-established harmony, neither in man himself, nor in culture, nor in society, nor in the Christian community. In all of them peace, as the unification of diverse recognised realities, is always something yet to be achieved. The remembrance of past misreadings helps to correct our present attitude—on condition, however, that we recognise in these misreadings a drama which goes beyond individuals. To overload them with an inventory of faults would only be an excuse for avoiding work to be done in the present. And more than any other human group, Christians are prone to do this, for they have an inveterate tendency to make moral judgements, misreading the inner laws and difficulties of mankind and his history. Furthermore, their yearning for an ideal Church prompts them either to idealise its past or to disclaim that past, without trying to elucidate it.

These remarks are meant to draw the following reflections into focus. The analysis of some areas of conflict between Christianity and mankind is an attempt to show that their resolution is the task of a Christian humanism which is always in the making and that by thus recognising the human element Christianity finds and accomplishes its own truth.

1. THE SUPERNATURAL AND THE HUMAN ORDER

By human order we mean everything which is included in the category of the human as such, what man has become explicitly aware of by formulating it as the basic freedom, or the rights of man. Christianity has contributed much to enlightening mán about himself and our culture is full of Christian ideas and values. However, a tension exists between the two poles of Christian orientation, the order of creation on the one hand and, on the other, the supernatural or divine initiative in history; and this tension has its repercussions on the complex and tormented relations of Christianity with culture.

(a) Suspicion or Conquest?

As we know, originally most cultures were penetrated by the sacred to the point that everything had a religious meaning and there did not even exist a word to designate the specific field which we distinguish as 'religion' Art, law, ethics, cosmology   were not only rooted in the sacred, they were premeated by it through and through. Biblical tradition has bound culture to religion even more closely, for by confessing the lordship of God over the cosmos and over man, it places everything directly under personal obedience to God. And Jesus Christ, the constant reference of all Christians, has no other interest but that of establishing the Kingdom of God. The fact that the autonomy of human realities has been won in all civilisations through much anguish is a measure of how much more formidable the inevitable and necessary separation between the human domains and the order of the faith would be in Christianity. What in theoretical thinking is called distinction takes on in real life the more conflictual aspects of a separation; it is achieved through the militant conquest of a new autonomy, against prior attachment.

One article cannot suffice to resume and interpret the immense history of cultural fields which, closely integrated in Christianity at the outset, have freed themselves from it, often in opposition to its wish for ascendancy, often also by revolting against it and seeking to destroy it in order to pass beyond it. Almost all the anti-Christian movements of ideas have risen against Chritianity precisely because they wanted to promote an idea of man which they considered more just and more exalted. Like the Christian message, they want to liberate man by truth. It should not be inferred from this that it is the fault of the Christian that his message is not heard, nor that the spirit of the unbeliever is clouded by a black passion. Neither one is absolutely good and sincere. If the divine Light seen in the darkness troubles all men, if some flee it because it reveals what is dark in them, it would none the less be unjust and presumptuous to accuse unbelievers of denying the light purely and simply. The revolutions in thought against the Christian faith prove that Christianity cannot boast 'of having a clear view of God, and of possessing him unveiled' (Pascal *Pensées*, ed. Lafuma, p. 427), because the biblical God is 'a God who hidest thyself' (Isaiah 45:15). To recognise human reality is to accept that man cannot seek truth without risks and that, by an inner necessity, truth is only found by contradictory movements.

We shall not harp back here to the restraints which the Church has exercised over the minds of men during the course of history. In proclaiming the right to religious freedom, Vatican II put into practical principle the theological principle already contained in the former Canon Law: 'No one may be compelled by force to embrace the Catholic faith.'

Not to compel is to give freedom to seek, thus also to make mistakes, for the moment when new truths are discovered, the true and the false are often inextricably mixed and no one has the absolute vision to separate them.

Committed Christians, especially those bearing ecclesiastical responsibilities, always risk suffocating the spirit, thus blocking the work of the Holy Spirit in a humanity which is exploring and developing. The awareness of having to keep intact truth and the dynamic of the faith carries with it the danger of becoming conservative and defensive. The eschatological awareness of the work of conversion to be done can lead to impatience that results in closing one's ears and impels one to the violent action of expelling anything that disturbs certainties. The parable of the tares among the wheat (Matt. 13:24-30) teaches us, however, that evangelical vigilance is only just if it does not violate the law of the human, which is also a law of divine providence.

The recognition of the human as criterion of true faith thus finds an essential domain of application in support for the sciences, whether philosophical, human or positive. This will always be the most difficult recognition of the human because it is the most dangerous, since it is a matter here of truth and since new truths are inevitably and confusedly intermingled with error. In our time it is without doubt the human sciences that present most questions to the Christian conscience. Two contradictory attitudes among decision-makers and theologians have been discernible. After some hesitation, some have resolutely opted for accepting sociology, psychology, and the new forms of hermeneutics. We can be glad of this, provided that the theoretical observations and concepts are not hastily diverted and distorted in order to be incorporated into a 'Christian vision' of man and the world. For too often, by integrating them and by trying to 'infiltrate' them, Christian thinkers do not allow themselves to be challenged by scientific facts, but manipulate them in order to retrieve them, although in all good faith. For example, we have heard a theologian declare that the psychoanalytic theory of the unconscious should be accepted because 'at the base of the unconscious is God'. And was not the favour which sociology enjoyed for a certain time in some ecclesiastical circles often owing to the rather naive hope of possessing an instrument of power? The desire to utilise the achievements of the sciences or of philosophy is legitimate on condition that, through them, one allows oneself genuinely to learn something about man and about his relations with the faith.

Others, after having undergone certain experiences, and scared by the crises provoked by the human sciences, nervously close the debate. The truth is that the sciences are to some extent animated by an atheist rationalism, and it is not by an historical accident that their promoters often oppose reason to faith. The boldness of discovery is imperialist by nature, so that the discovery, for example, of the psychological or sociological conditions or causes of certain forms of religion tends to lead spontaneously to the assumption that the whole question has been covered and to the relegation of religion to what is assumed to explain it. The sciences discover hitherto unsuspected determinisms or conditionings and each discovery about the faith contradicts a way of thinking which was bound to the faith. The work of sifting has still to be done on the shifting frontiers of science. Having learned that one cannot utilise the human sciences neutrally, all the less so as they tend to say more than they know, religious institutions prefer not to expose themselves to a debate which seems too risky. But is this not paying lip service to the order of creation without agreeing to it in spirit?

(b) The temptation of supernaturalism

There is a certain type of Christian language which speaks as though God were transparent in the events of the world or the Church. Spiritual texts and speeches teem with expressions which, though not false in themselves, betray a tendency to supernaturalise, that is, to attribute to a perceptible divine initiative what is also an initiative of man. The intention to commit oneself to the religious life is called a vocation by God. Attraction to Christian conversion is an appeal from God. The difficulties on the path chosen are trials sent by God. It happens that pious enthusiasm is turned into apostolic propaganda: in the swift election of Pope John Paul I rejoicing believers and bishops saw a striking sign of the intervention of the Holy Spirit among the Cardinals.

Such language can prove a heavy burden on men's shoulders. Many of the called or chosen have been tormented by the guilt of disbelief. How can one in fact seek to clarify whether 'one has a vocation' if the idea came very early, inculated by recitals of heroism or in imitation of an admired example and if Christian discourse gives it the authority of a divine voice comparable to the word of Jahweh addressing the prophets? The pressure exerted by spiritual leaders whose faith can blind their common sense contributes by ambiguities to confusing the sincere search of candidates. They are confronted by a dilemma, unable to realise that this dilemma is unreal; 'One can only love God totally or not at all.'

These few examples illustrate the difficulty is inherent in the very position of Christianity which consists in holding together believing trust in the action of the living God and the conviction that God does not manipulate man like a spiritual automaton. The distinction is all the more difficult as we are the heirs of a spiritual tradition according to which all the vicissitudes of life refer directly back to the divine light and power. It is the proper right of faith to perceive God in every event and for that faith everything is grace. It would actually be lacking in faith to deny it. For the Christian life is totally grafted onto the supernatural order and this is all embracing. The fact remains that man is still man, with his understanding, his illusions, the effects of his unconscious memories on his life and also on his religious conceptions. The progressive emancipation of critical consciousness and the more systematic explorations of historical, psychological and sociological determinisms no longer permit the idea that any religious intention is simply supernatural and that any thinking towards God is supernaturally inspired. What has altered through this is not the faith that everything is grace; it is the manner of conceiving the connection between the two orders, nature and the supernatural. In a concrete way of interpreting and acting, the principle 'grace supposes nature', without being denied, should be understood as a compenetration. Discussions on grace still tend to give too much of an impression of a nature-supernature parallelism, similar to the psycho-physiological parallelism.

Let us consider by way of example the language of the mystics, not to take it to task for its supernaturalism, but to illustrate the need to distinguish and to combine the supernatural and the human. God visits them, and after having palpably dwelt within them in the initial experience of union, he educates their faith and their love. He leads them into the desert to purify their faith and their attachment to tangible experiences and imaginary or intellectual displays. God, however, lightens their suffering in one of naked faith by gratifying them with visions. Sufferings or ecstatic experiences, all these vicissitudes and all these experiences are attributed to divine initiative. The language of the mystics is, however, not that of a raving supernaturalism, for if they teach the mystic way, it is because faith itself is the common beginning of that path and offers the possibility of embarking on it. And they are striving constantly to discern whether the thoughts, feelings or visions come from God or from the spirit of evil. By requiring sustained vigilance and systematic effort, mystics attribute an essential function to the human; it must surrender to divine power in order to receive it when it manifests itself and bestows itself. This does not hinder them from interpreting as directly supernatural phenomena that in our age we can put down to the domain of psychological logic. Their experinces of the silence of God, their moments of ecstatic possession and their visions obey natural laws which are explained by psychology. The recognition of truly human processes underlying mystical phenomena does not imply a reduction of the latter to the purely human. In fact, the hidden dynamisms which psychology reveals do not produce the presence of God but they do condition its modalities: silence, visions, brilliant manifestation or intuition of lasting indwelling. Our more explicit knowledge of the human does not naturalise the supernatural, but obliges us always to see it in conjunction with the human. In this sense the supernatural, in profound accord with man, penetrates him and is not confined to apparently irrational manifestations.

The refusal to recognise the compenetration of the human and the supernatural distorts the Christian faith by means of two opposing attitudes. On the one hand, there are those who take delight in seeking and exhibiting tangible manifestations of the divine Spirit. It is the danger which, in our age, lies in wait for certain charismatic groups. It is believed that the miraculous power of the Holy Spirit can be perceived in the so-called 'speaking with tongues'. It is thought that the Spirit will miraculously bring deliverance from psychopathological suffering. It is proclaimed that with God everything is possible. The narcissistic self-centredness which affects such spiritual exaltation can be embarrassing. We fear above all that these enthusiasms interpreted in a miraculous way will cause work on the natural resistance which man and the world offer to the spirit of God to be misunderstood. And the infatuation with anticipated eschatology causes participation in social and cultural human realities to be despised or at least neglected, which Christianity also has a vocation to promote and open to God.

On the other hand, there are others who distrust too much mystical or charismatic seeking and experiences. They are afraid that these will evolve outside doctrine and institutionalised activities. They closely identify the supernatural with practices regulated by universal prescriptions. This attitude, which causes suspicion to cramp creative freedoms, also results from a cleft between the human and the supernatural. In fact, if it were admitted that God is joined to the human as it really is, with its very variable contexts, situations and initiatives, they would be given more latitude.

(c) Consequences affecting sacramental practice

The effects of supernaturalism on the sacraments have been disastrous and we are still suffering from its ruinous consequences. The drop in church attendance in Western Christianity is without any doubt due in part to the degeneration of forms of worship in the old liturgy. The sacraments, which theology calls the 'instruments of grace', had taken a really instrumental form, which reduces the human to a minimum in the execution of the sacrament. The part played by 'liturgical renewal' has been essential. Much more than aesthetics, pedagogical adaptation or fidelity to an ancient tradition, what is at stake in the recognition or exclusion of the human as mediation of divine action is theological truth.

Sacramental practice should be analysed as an anthropologist would, who would shelve the theology of grace and refer only to what the rite might signify in the Christian context. Let us pinpoint just a few elements, taking as a model the extreme case, as was formerly generally the custom. While the essential sacraments, baptism and the Eucharist, consist of highly significant physical gestures, physical expression is in practice reduced to the gesture which is technically necessary to 'receive the sacrament'. 'Celebration' is carried out in a dreary recitation of 'chants'. The organisation of space contradicts the elementary laws of symbolism and of the formation of a community. People are invited to confess their sins while the necessary predisposition to believe is not yet formed, simply in order to perform a rite of transition between the exterior and the interior. A long inventory of ritual nonsense can be summed up by the formula: a strictly codified formalism eliminates the natural power of expression and the initiatory process. The underlying reason for this is in the theological polarisation in regard to a grace which is supposed to be given by sacramental 'means'. Such an outlook then arouses a permanent concern for moralising exhortation in order for the faithful to be in a state worthy of the divine gift. Nowhere else, without a doubt, has the division between the supernatural and the human so perverted attitudes. Nothing, moreover, should associate them so closely for, precisely because they are rites, the sacraments contain humanly symbolic actions and concerns. They prolong the incarnation by means of what God is operating in it and through what is humanly true and meaningful.

2. ETHICS AND SPIRITUALITY

In these two areas the renewal of the Church is striking. While in the not too distant past the ethics taught related exclusively to discipline, to perfection and to personal charity, in our times the Church has also proclaimed its social demands and has committed itself to movements for freeing man in his humanity. Spiritual formation no longer imposes from on high an ideal of Christian perfection, as a supra-human idea which has broken free from the human condition. We need only think of the modern training given to priests and religious or of the many opportunities the laity have to learn: it is in real life that one progressively learns to discover and inwardly absorb the evangelical principles of a life which conforms to the faith. It would then be pointless to keep harping on about the caricatures of former times. However, we should reflect on certain errors committed by Christianity which reveal inherent difficulties in its relations with the human.

The obsession with sexuality has been the moral neurosis of Christianity. Consciences have been so tormented by a mistaken preoccupation with the erotic that it has taken the lion's share in examinations of conscience and confessions! This massive culpabilisation of sexuality, which has fostered so much sterile psychological suffering, reveals on analysis a profound distrust of pleasure. Pleasure was opposed by an ethics of duty, a word which seemed to sum up moral good. The mother was also idealised for her devotion, as though she were not more naturally a real mother if she also enjoyed her motherhood. Sexuality was in fact only admitted if procreation as service to the community justified the pleasurable part of it. The cultivation of gratuitous pleasure did not seem to be capable of coming to terms with a Christian attitude.

How are we to understand this grim war against sexuality? The moral preoccupation of the Church with family and society certainly partly explains it. It saw that uncontrolled sexuality breaks up the family and dangerously disrupts the organised world. More profoundly, the Church has felt that carnal pleasure is an experience so intense that in itself it does not lead to the desire to find happiness in God, but risks, on the contrary, absorbing that desire. God and pleasure are not in natural harmony. Psychoanalysis even shows that unconscious reasons cause man to feel them to be in competition with one another. However, if sexuality is an essential dimension of human existence, the task of Christian education should be to teach how to pass beyond this opposition, to make of pleasure a form of love and of human love a symbolic participation in the religious joy which the proclamation of the Kingdom brings. It is not our intention, however, to glorify sexuality, as some forms of Christian discussion do, by designating it the place of religious experience. This again is to deny the human by an abstract integration into an unreal religious unity.

For those who know how sexual life can broaden existence and confirm love and what are the baneful consequences of its disturbance, the laws of the ecclesiastical authorities are really incomprehensible. At the moment they seem to be the gravest denial of the human. The Church loses thereby not only its authority in a matter which is essential to civilisation, but its misreading of human reality renders its very religious message suspect.

The recognition of the human must not, however, lead to a misreading of Christian positions. The renunciation of sexuality represents a way of life, from the eschatological perspective, which allows the will of God to be sustained and acted on. This form of Christian existence does not diminish man, for as individual option it promotes one of the human possibilities that faith makes available. But this type of Christian life becomes humanly and religiously false when it is presented as the ideal pattern. In such a case, the profound originality of Christianity is being misread. According to the revelation of Jesus Christ, God comes to man as he really is. Man must not abandon his human condition to find God, for the very reason that the kingdom of God comes to him. No world-God dualism is compatible with faith in the incarnation. The 'flight from the world' can be the obvious path for some. To reconcile the world and God is a difficult task for any Christian. But to preach flight from the world as the Christian truth, as was done formerly by a dominant form of spirituality, is to reintroduce the dividing line between the human and God when the revelation of Jesus brings them together.

Translated by Della Couling

Edward Schillebeeckx

Christian Identity and Human Integrity

A GREAT deal of what is offered with a decorative description as 'humanism' has a barely hidden ideological character. This is quite clear from slogans that can easily be found in books and articles. On the one hand, for example, it is possible to read: 'What is Christian is human and what is human is Christian'. On the other, I have recently read this statement: 'What is communist is human and what is human is communist'. It would not be difficult to find other examples of similar statements. A misuse of ideological language of this kind should not, however, cause us to overlook the real question of the relationship between 'humanity' and what is proposed by religion and philosophy as their most profound convictions concerning human life. We should rather accept it as a warning against prematurely making syntheses and identifications.

Whatever wealth it may contain, Christian faith is undoubtedly concerned with 'humanity' and certainly with men and women who believe in God. No one, however, possesses exclusive rights over true humanity, which is something that concerns all men. In any case, 'humanity' is an abstract term. It exists only in very diverse cultural forms, although this may be on the basis of a fundamentally identical biogenetical substratum. Any hegemony of a definite culture is therefore pernicious, because it is tainted with 'regionalism' and imperialism.

1. THE DANGER OF BEING THEOLOGICALLY SQUINT-EYED

One encounters more pseudo-problems in theology in the case of pairs of concepts such as 'humanity and Christianity', 'human freedom and grace', 'evolution and creation' and even 'self-liberation and justification by grace alone' than in almost any other area. Quite frequently opposing concepts which in fact point to something in reality are projected *as such* into that reality so that they become two opposing or parallel realities which have to be dialectically reconciled with each other. This is, of course, a hopeless task, a good example of which is the struggle about grace that took place in the past in the Catholic Church. This and other struggles were about problems that could not be solved.

At the level of concepts and their linguistic expression, 'humanity' and 'Christianity' (or approaching the kingdom of God) are certainly placed alongside each other. They are frequently equated with each other and then included within the same proposition, as though they were two distinct realities—for example, 'grace and freedom'. The question, however, is whether they can be taken cumulatively. A good human action, performed in freedom, is grace in the concrete, although it at the same time transcends that freedom. A Christian can in this way experience a case of acquired 'humanity' as 'Christian'.

In such statements, the language of faith and empirical and analytical language point to the same reality, but, in both language games, the pertinence of each and its formal approach have to be respected and should not be confused. If they are confused, it is as if the ace of hearts were thrown down on the chess board—meaningless and absurd gesture. (The image is Wittgenstein's.) The theologian who simply studies the causes, the legal aspects and the inner structures of 'human' actions is not concerning himself formally with theology; he is rather reconnoitring the approaches to the territory which he intends to explore and about which he proposes to say something 'Christian'. His exploration of that territory or the 'material object', even if he is, as a theologian, dependent on other sciences, is for him a theological task in the sense that, without that reconnoitring, the formally theological task is meaningless and something that is done in a vacuum. It is therefore important that he should not forget that the first reconnoitring of the approaches should include other and not purely theological authorities. The theologian who is in fact concerned with these approaches to the territory in which the struggle for salvation or its opposite takes place must first listen very carefully to human experiences and especially to experiences of contrast and also to what other human sciences may be able to tell him. As Thomas Aquinas pointed out, 'multa praecognoscere (theologus) oportet'[1]—before the theologian can act as a theologian, he has a great deal of reconnoitring to do. At that level, it is very important indeed to listen to men and women to what they want to achieve as humanity. In other words, interdisciplinarity is necessary.

The theologian, however, only enters the formally and distinctively theological territory, in which his own distinctive authority can be brought into play, when he includes the territory that he has already reconnoitred within a different language game, asks different questions and looks at it from a different point of view. The language that he has to use here is that of faith, which is one that speaks about salvation coming from God in Jesus the Christ. It is, in other words, not a question of speaking about a different reality, but of speaking about the same reality which has already been reconnoitred in a 'human' way. Interdisciplinarity no longer helps in this case and indeed, it is no longer appropriate. If we tried to bring it into play, we should inevitably be looking asquint at what appears on the one hand as 'human' and on the other as 'Christian'. Two divergent language games are involved, because the reality itself has many dimensions which cannot all be expressed at the same time in a single language game. The material that has first been analysed by a theologian is then decoded by him in the light of faith. He treats that material as a text that has to be interpreted according to the grammar of Christian hope and faith in God, who is the source of universal, all-embracing and definitive salvation. The question that then confronts the theologian is whether a coming or an approach of the kingdom of God can be detected in this particular human action performed to achieve greater humanity. (He does not look for *the* coming, but for *a* coming of the kingdom in it.)

2. THE ABSOLUTE CHARACTER OF COMMITMENT TO FAITH AND ITS DISTINCTIVE FORM

Speaking about God as the one who saves men and sets them free has to be done in a 'second language game'. It is in fact a speaking about something that has already been discussed in a 'first discourse'. What has first been seen as a 'human reality' is discussed by Christians in the light of its 'Christian content' or the opposite, its value as the absence of salvation. It does not, however, in any way follow from the character of faith as a 'second discourse' that faith and theology are always too late. This belatedness is not the fault of faith and theology as such. It can be attributed to the fact that believers and theologians often arrive too late when the phenomena, which have to be made ready to be discussed theologically in a second discourse, in fact take place. Christians may well have the searchlight of faith at their disposal, but they do not always recognise that a new object is appearing in our human experience and that this requires a theological interpretation. Anyone who arrives too late when the phenomenon takes place is also, of course, too late to throw light on it with the purpose of enabling Christians to practise more effectively.

Theology is speaking about what is absolute but occurs within the relative, in other words, within human praxis in history. This relative matter is, of course, often a matter of life and death. Theology expresses the ultimate and transcendent commitment of men in historical praxis, since, for the believer, human activity in the concrete, including political activity, is always either positively or negatively, but never neutrally, related to the coming of the kingdom of God. Although that kingdom must be realised in and through definite acts performed by men, it can never be reduced to a particular praxis. This does not mean that the absolute and total character of commitment to faith cannot be expressed in a definite or very particular human praxis within a particular historical situation and that it cannot be expressed in this way again and again in particular contexts. We are ultimately judged on the basis of whether we have given food to the hungry and drink to the thirsty (Matt. 25:40).

Christianity is therefore essentially concerned with human integrity, that is, with being whole or with salvation. This does not point to a reduction of 'Christianity' simply to 'humanity', but it does constitute the concrete historical state within which Christianity can be given form. The absolute character of Christian faith in God is therefore revealed in what is particular, historical and relative, in other words, in historical humanity, even though humanity and Christianity are not identical. Anyone who wants to experience what is absolute in a pure state or as 'available unwrapped' will therefore never be confronted with it—or he will only be confronted with idols. We can only reach 'God's Word' within the confines of our cultural and material possibilities and our own historical sphere of life. The absolute is only made manifest in the greater and smaller phenomena of every day. In everyday life, it is made clear that what concerns man also concerns God and also that God's affair can also concern us in the greater and the smaller context of the life of society and the individual. It is precisely this that the theologian aims to decode—that is why he is a theologian.

We can therefore conclude our preliminary considerations by saying that the transcendence of Christian salvation and faith in God cannot be used as a pretext for an attitude that is neutral with regard to furthering humanity or that is politically neutral. Whatever its content may be, what is Christian and universally human can never be realised outside a definite and particular human context. Since the eighteenth century, we have learnt from the abstract humanity of the Enlightenment how ideological the bourgeois idea of the 'universally human' reality was.

For the Christian, it is certainly a question of the relationship between God and man, in which the world and human history are as it were inserted by God between us and himself as a translation of his inner address, as the medium in and through which man's attention is explicitly drawn to this inner speaking and finally as the space within which man can respond, in his life, to this invitation.

Christians are right to interpret certain actions, including political and social actions, as Christians, that is, as soteriological, even if humanists call the same praxis humanist, in the non-Christian sense. A definite socio-political praxis cannot, after all, be regarded as exempt from its own particular rationality, substance and specific aims; in that sense, there is no action in the world that the Christian is able to claim entirely for himself. The dream, vision or promise of a better society, a fuller life for humanity and an environment 'with a human face', however, forms an essential part of the essential Christian Gospel, which is the message of the kingdom of a God who is concerned with humanity and who wants men who are similarly concerned with humanity. Christian faith is therefore intimately connected with an ethos of humanity. The criteria for social and political action in the concrete cannot, it is true, be derived from the 'utopia' of the kingdom of God, but this ethical action, which has to be judged according to its own criteria, includes the believer in the theological virtues of faith, hope and charity. A political praxis that is directed towards a more human environment is therefore for Christians as well the socio-political content of Christian hope in terms of historical praxis. For the believer, then, what is political and social cannot be reduced to merely political and social components, since there is more at stake than simply those parts. And it is with this 'more' that is at stake that the theologian is concerned.

3. SPEAKING ABOUT GOD IN THE CONTEXT OF THE HUMAN SEARCH FOR LIBERATION

(a) The Religious Question of Salvation

Our ideas and our expectations of salvation, liberation and human happiness are always the result of our concrete experience and our reflection about the reality itself of misery, alienation and the absence of salvation. They are the result of an accumulation of negative experiences in a history of suffering that has lasted for centuries but that is also shot through with flashes of meaningful experience, happiness, partial experiences of salvation, meaning and salvation, even though that history has for the most part been one of unfulfilled expectations, evil and guilt. In the long run, what emerges from this pattern, which is culturally and even geographically diverse, is a vision of what is regarded as a true, happy and good human state for society and the individual. The constant human longing for happiness, salvation and justice, which is again and again subjected to the criticism of facts, but which is constantly and paradoxically reborn from the felt sense of non-sense, therefore inevitably acquires in many different forms, the emphasis of 'redemption from' or 'liberation from' suffering and alienation and at the same time of 'entering a new world'.

What is particularly striking in this human process of experience of the absence of salvation and partial experience of salvation in humanity is that a particular people's own ideas of salvation are not only an attempt to fathom the depths of human suffering, but also an effort to interpret the causes, origins and consequences of that suffering. In the ancient world, this experience of the absence of salvation always has, on the basis of the human depths of the history of suffering that in theory cannot be fathomed and in praxis cannot ever be completely eliminated, a *religious* dimension. This is also the case not only in ancient society, but in the spontaneous experience of all peoples. In the spontaneous view of men, the absence of salvation and alienation cannot be, either theoretically or practically, measured on a human scale. For this reason, men's expectations of salvation acquire a *religious name*. Humanity came, in the past, to expect salvation 'from God'. Despite all experiences of the contrary, mankind has learnt to expect gentleness and mercy in the deepest heart of reality.

(b) The Non-Religious Question of Salvation

What, however, do we encounter in our contemporary, so-called 'secularised' society? What in the past seemed to concern religious people almost exclusively has now come to preoccupy all those who specialise in or are influenced by the human sciences —

everyone is looking for healing or human salvation and liberation from enslaved societies. It is hardly possible to deny that, apart from any distinction between faith and reason, the question of a sound and liveable humanity is, as a question, more central than ever before for the whole of mankind and that the reply to that question is given all the more urgently and persistently the more aware we become of our own human failings, the more we recognise that we are treated inadequately and the more sensitive we become to our experience of fragments of human healing and self-liberation. This question of salvation and liberation and of a truly liveable humanity is, however, always asked within actual conditions of disintegration, alienation and hurtful human encounters. The question of salvation and liberation is, of course, the fundamental question posed by all religions. It has, however, now become the great stimulus in the whole of contemporary human existence and, what is more, it is asked outside the sphere of all human religions. It is no longer religions that explicitly systematise the theme of human salvation. The question of salvation is no longer simply a religious and theological theme of redemption and liberation. On the contrary, it is now the driving force of our contemporary history and that, of course, includes our 'profane' history. It is clearer than it has ever been before that human history is the place where decisions and, what is more, explicitly conscious decisions are made about man's healing and liberation.

We may therefore draw a third conclusion in the course of this story. It is this. Anyone who wishes to speak meaningfully about God and Christian redemption must do this within the context of the contemporary theme of salvation and liberation. It is ultimately a question as to whether we can show that there is, in the liberation and the emancipation of men who are seeking a better humanity, something that is absolute or the absolute reality itself, in other words, whether we can show that what concerns man also concerns God. It is only then that we shall be able to show that God's affair can also concern us. If this is true, this religious dimension of our human life also calls for an expression or an articulation and a liturgical celebration of thanksgiving. It also requires a tangibly human expression to be given, in various circumstances, to this mystery in a praxis of the kingdom of God that everyone is able to recognise.

(c) God is Promise

The Christian faith in creation has a critical and productive power with regard to both pessimistic and optimistic views of human salvation which can be realised in human history and society. (These views are, of course, ultimately unrealistic.) As I have already said above, what in the past only concerned religions is now a shared task confronting all men, even those who are not religious. The conclusion that has from time to time been drawn from this datum is this. If we accept that we owe the introduction of many human values to the Christian tradition, it has at the same time to be admitted that those values have now come to be shared by all men. We are consequently able now, while thanking Christianity for the service that it has rendered to humanity in the past, to let Christian faith itself go. I, however, believe that this would be a very minimal way of viewing the inexhaustible potential for expectation and inspiration that is contained within the Christian faith in creation and the activity of the Spirit of God. It is historically verifiable that inspirations that were originally religious gradually become universal in humanity as a whole, in other words, that they enter the secular sphere. As a demand and an argument for totality, however, this is a disastrous impasse, above all because of our own finite nature, which may be regarded as a definition of 'secularity'. For the Christian, this finite nature can never be separated from the absolute creative presence of God and for this reason it can never be secularised and it can never cease to exist. This creative, saving presence of God is an inexhaustible source of expectation and future hope which transcends the potential for action of the finite.

In the Christian tradition of experience, God is regarded, not as the 'power of life and death', but rather as 'pure positivity'. He is, in other words, 'a God of the living' who wants all men to be saved and set free. The absolute dividing line between God and ourselves is not God's, but our dividing line. God's free Being is therefore an inexhaustible Promise for man. His name is 'Promise'. The Christian faith in creation includes the fact that God loves us without limits or conditions. His love for us is unmerited, unconditional and unlimited. Creation is an act of God, who in this way on the one hand places us unconditionally in our finite, non-divine distinctive nature which is destined to true humanity and, on the other, places himself in disinterested love as our God, our happiness and salvation and the highest content of true humanity. God creates man freely for the happiness and salvation of men themselves, but even within this act he wants, in sovereign freedom, to be, in the deepest sense, the happiness and salvation of human life. He is a God of people, our God. This, in a nutshell, is the Christian faith in creation. But how does it work out?

How it works out is clear from the history that is made, for good or evil, by men themselves. Faith in creation means that God's Being is revealed. This in turn means that who God is, that is, the distinctive mode of being of God's state of being God, is determined or conditioned by nothing, but is revealed in and through the whole of our history. Christians therefore call God the Lord of that history. The risky venture of creatively giving life to men and women is, seen from God's point of view, an act of trust in man and his history that sets up no conditions or guarantees on man's side. Creation is therefore a blank cheque for which only God himself acts as surety. It is an act of trust which gives the man who believes in God the courage to believe in word and deed that the kingdom of God, that is human happiness and salvation, is, despite many experiences of the absence of salvation, *de facto* in course of preparation for man, in the power of God's creative action which moves men to realise it.

This is why God, who is the reliable one, is, in his freedom, constantly surprising man. According to the book of Revelation, he is the one 'who is and who was and who is to come' (Rev. 1:8; 4:8). God's Being is unchanging. It is not that of a creature. It is therefore, on the basis of his eternal and absolute freedom, permanently new for finite man. Because his act of creation is an act of his eternal and absolutely free Being, his absolute nature or non-relative nature is at the same time relational, that is, it is related in absolute freedom that is determined or conditioned by nothing to his creature, man in the world. In creating, God takes sides with everything that is created, that is, with everything that is vulnerable because it is contingent. In that way, what concerns man also concerns God, although this does not in any sense diminish man's responsibility for his own history.

It is clearly very difficult for men to believe in a divine Being who in complete freedom determines what, who and how 'he'—or 'it' or she' (human words fail here)—that is, God, really is. Yet this is certainly faith in God. It is only in a very limited way that is restricted by all kinds of conditions that we human beings can freely determine what, who and how we ourselves want to be in accordance with our own plan or view of life. Even there, we often fail to a very great extent. God's Being, on the other hand, is precisely as God wishes it to be, without any elusive or independent remainder. He freely determines what he, as God, wants to be for himself and for us. He does not do this arbitrarily, but in unconditional love. This is the essence of the Christian confession of faith.

God's Being was revealed to us in Jesus. God the creator, who is the reliable one, is the love that sets man free in a way that both fulfils and transcends all human, personal, social and political expectations. God's Being is Promise for man.

That is why our human history can never replace the inexhaustible potential of our faith in creation for expectation and inspiration. It releases reserves of hope and energy in the believer which cannot simply be reduced to purely human expectations. In this sense, man can only realise the promise of his own being as grace. As Ignatius of Antioch rightly said: 'Only when I am come thither shall I be truly a man'.[2] Ultimately, humanity is an eschatological gift of the Spirit, the fruit of God's liberating love in Jesus Christ—a fruit which God allows to ripen in and through the historical praxis of men, while he himself always transcends this in a sovereign manner.

The indefinable nature of definitive salvation and eschatological freedom, that is, of the *Humanum* that is sought and found only fragmentarily and yet always threatened, can therefore only be expressed in the symbolic language of metaphorical speech that goes further than all conceptuality. There are three great 'metaphors', expressed in many different sounds, in the New Testament which suggest the complete *Humanum*. The first of these is the definitive salvation or radical liberation of all men into a brotherly and sisterly community or society where the master-slave relationship no longer exists. This is known in the New Testament as the 'kingdom of God'. The second is known in the New Testament as *sarx* or 'flesh'. It is the perfect salvation and happiness of the individual person within the perfect society, known in the Christian tradition as 'resurrection of the flesh', that is, the resurrection of the human person into his corporeality. The third 'metaphor' is the fulfilment of the 'ecological environment' that is so necessary for human life that is suggested in the biblical idea of the 'new heaven and new earth'.

These three metaphors of visions orientate the activity of Christians in this world in a direction that is in no way vague and undefined, but is very clear and definite. (It is indicated by the dynamism of the symbols themselves.) This is so, even though they cannot, without being mediated in a human context, ever provide a direct blueprint for personal and socio-political action here and now.

4. THE WAY OF SUFFERING THROUGH AND FOR OTHERS

It should be clear from what I have already said that all religious and Christian speaking about God is at the same time a critical and productive speaking about man and that religious and Christian speaking about man is also a speaking about God. It is precisely because God's Being is 'love of man' that these two aspects cannot be separated. This inevitably means that what is specifically religious and Christian is essentially concerned with what is specifically human. Christianity cannot be Christian if it does not take 'humanity' seriously—humanity is precisely the place where God is sought and encountered. This insight into Christian faith is provided by creation and Christology as realities of Christian experience (and only secondarily as 'theological themes'). Our existence in time is given shape as today, yesterday and tomorrow, that is, as trust, memory and expectation, by this 'hermeneutical circle' of protology and eschatology, that is, of memory and expectation.

When Ignatius of Antioch wrote his well-known words: 'Only when I am come-thither shall I be truly a man', he did that on the eve of his approaching death as a martyr. True humanity is also concerned with the way of suffering through and for others. This is clearly the fundamental theme of the gospel of Mark, the first letter of Peter and the epistle to the Hebrews. It can even be seen as the basic theme of the whole of the New Testament. In this sense, what is 'Christian' assumes a 'human' form in its heights and depths, but at the same time this is a humanity that is able to trust in God's absolute saving presence both in suffering and impotence and in prosperity and adversity. The active search, which always takes place within a cultural, social and even geographical context, for the incomprehensible mystery of the ultimate *Humanum* in fact merges into the mystery of the 'suffering righteous man', who has been entrusted to us in the living example of the eschatological 'suffering prophet' Jesus, the 'Holy and Righteous one' (Acts 3:14) who was rightly called the 'Son of God'. It is here that the 'power'—the biblical *dunamis*—of defenceless and disarming love is revealed. The suffering of our fellow-men is experienced in Jesus' appearance as a task. His death is the result of the irresistible power of goodness. We can either accept this goodness or we can oppose it, but only by torturing and disposing of a man like Jesus, in an act which bears witness, indirectly but in a very real way, to our own impotence.

This, then, is the essence of the Jewish and Christian testimony that is evident in the Old Testament and confirmed in the New. Suffering through and for others, to which our faith bears witness, can therefore be seen as an expression of the unconditional validity of a praxis of doing good and of resistance to evil and innocent suffering. The man who does not limit his commitment to the suffering of others in any way is bound, even now, to pay for it sooner or later with his own death. It is precisely with this that Jesus 'reconciled himself'. He was consistent in his own commitment to man as God's concern. In 'this world', standing up for 'what concerns man' means in fact suffering for goodness. The self-realisation of humanism, which does not take this datum sufficiently into account, is not realistic and ultimately not even 'humanist'.

It is difficult to deny that the Christian creed places great emphasis on Jesus' death and resurrection and says nothing about his message and the praxis of his life, although we know that, in view of the power of 'this world', Jesus' death can only be understood in the light of his life and message. His death and resurrection are in fact the summary of his prophetic life and message. We are able to see why this is so as soon as we begin seriously to consider his life and message in the light of the New Testament. What we see there is that Jesus does not speak of what is human in the abstract (in ancient, feudal or bourgeois society or in any other form). He speaks of the rich and the poor, the oppressed and the oppressors and others in the concrete and he takes sides. The gospels were written in reaction against 'mythological' and in fact ideological tendencies which later traced the whole Christian creed back to the death and resurrection of Jesus, while suppressing his life and message. Such tendencies always run the risk of making Jesus' message of the kingdom of God, which is so concerned with men, the object of criticism. Political dictatorships led by so-called Christians, who see themselves as 'defenders of Western Christianity' and who celebrate the death and resurrection of Jesus Christ on Sundays, would be impossible if those dictators were really conscious of the fact that Jesus' death and resurrection are based on the life and message of a God who is concerned with humanity and with man, as Jesus shows him to us in human history. 'Orthodoxy' becomes a mere mockery of the Gospel and the Christian tradition in such cases.

In fact, many men have, because of their irrational impulses, which are often expressed politically, the most grotesque expectations of God. One such expectation is that, if you give yourself entirely to God and are exclusively preoccupied with God's affair as something that concerns man, nothing other than God exists for you—God the great bird who swallows up the smaller birds—with the result that you are bound to ignore yourself and the world that God created and loves. But the fact that God's affair is above all a concern for man, that God makes the affair of man his own affair and that this is precisely what is meant by what is known in the Gospels as the 'kingdom of God' is something that goes far beyond all men's expectations. If men think in a purely human way about God, this can result in bizarre and humanly degrading theories and practices. Men have often enough made human sacrifices in their attempts to honour God. This occurred frequently in the past, but is it any different now? Does not the absence of salvation and the presence of so much suffering reveal itself again and again in the contemporary world under the banner of God and religion? Has not at least one Christology made Jesus into a God who does not show mercy to men until the blood of the one who is greatly loved flows? Jesus, however, said: 'If you are conscious of God's approach, do not be afraid' (see Mark 4:35, etc.). God is above all a God of people. He is a God who thinks of human sacrifice as an 'abomination' (see Lev. 18:21-30; 20:1-5). God is a fire, certainly, but he is a fire that burnt the bush without consuming it (Exod. 3:2).

God's choice for 'humanism' would appear to be directed towards a 'humanism of the rejected': 'Blessed are the poor, . . . those who hunger, . . . those who mourn' (Matt. 5:3-12), precisely because they do not oppress or reject anyone, but are themselves rejected. He showed his love for us 'while we were yet sinners' (Rom. 5:8).

Translated by David Smith

Notes

1. Thomas Aquinas *Summa Contra Gentiles* I, 4.
2. Ignatius of Antioch *Ad Romanos* VI, 2; see *Early Christian Writings. The Apostolic Fathers*, translated by Maxwell Staniforth (Harmondsworth 1968) p. 105.

Dietmar Mieth

Autonomy of Ethics— Neutrality of the Gospel?

THE PROPOSAL that humanness should be a criterion of Christianity calls for a process of rethinking in the Church. Christianity has often put forward a specific view of what is human, but presented it as something which made no sense outside a Christian framework. If the 'human' is to become a criterion, there must be prior agreement about the term before dogmatic anthropology gets to work.

A particular difficulty in this process of rethinking is that Christianity is now being asked to accept a criterion with which it has often been confronted since the Enlightenment as a criterion of the 'post-Christian' era: the value of the Christian faith, in this view, lies in the extent to which it promotes the humanity of human beings and, ideally, is absorbed by this.

Finally, this process of rethinking means the surrender of ethics to autonomous reason.[1] Religion, it seems, may still give the answer to Kant's question, 'What may we hope for?', but it is the practical reason which answers the question, 'What should we do?' From this one conclusion is that of Thomas Mann: 'I believe in goodness, not in religion,' which transforms all religion into moral hope. The other is that of the Christian, who asks himself, 'Isn't it enough to be a good person? Why am I a Christian?'

The question is all-absorbing. Is Christian humanism Christianity perfected in humanism or, as some claim, in a derivative of humanism, socialism? Or is the humanness of Christianity something distinct, something different from other religious and non-religious concepts of the human? In that case the use of humanness as a criterion of Christian existence would be circular or tautological: we would have already appropriated the criterion by which we measured ourselves. A humanistic criterion, all right, but one in turn judged by a *Christian* humanism. Autonomous ethics, certainly, but in turn safely sheltered under a theonomy which enables us to distinguish in advance between true and false autonomy. The question becomes even more pressing when one takes into account the differences between a European 'autonomous ethics in a Christian context' and a Latin American ethics of liberation. In the latter the reincorporation of ethical autonomy into Christianity is not a goal, but nor is it a premise. Christian action for liberation analyses, judges and acts 'by faith', i.e. in terms of the fundamental religious option of partiality for the disadvantaged. J. Ratzinger has perceptively observed that in current Christian ethics there is a conflict between autonomy on the one hand and religious orthopraxy on the other.[2]

32

The core of the problem is this. Theological ethics today refuses to abandon two premises. On the one hand it asserts the ethical relevance, and so denies the ethical neutrality, of the Gospel, and on the other it insists on maintaining the autonomy of ethics, since this seems to it to be the only model for maintaining the 'morality of autonomy' or, if the term is preferred, 'the ethic of freedom' made possible by the Gospel. By maintaining both premises, I wish to argue, one can reconcile them.

Before demonstrating this, I shall consider the criticisms of the alternatives at present offered as basic models in Christian ethics, the model of 'autonomous morality' and the model of 'revealed morality'. What is at issue in both cases is not just a method of argumentation in theological ethics, but an understanding of ethics as such.

1. THE BEGINNING: CRITICISM OF THE NEO-SCHOLASTIC DISTINCTION BETWEEN REASON AND
REVELATION

The neo-scholastic basis of moral theology at the turn of the century was, crudely, the following: There are two sources of moral knowledge, natural knowledge through reason and supernatural revelation, manifested in scripture. Both sources were left with their autonomy, but placed in a hierarchy: revelation was greater than reason. The authority for both sources was the tradition of the Church's magisterium, a point constantly emphasised in statements of the magisterium down to the time of Pius XII.

I make no attempt to claim here that this position was not argued in a much more complex form than that presented here, but the implications of the approach remained: there was a twofold order of humanness. One order rested on 'natural laws' of morality recognisable by anyone; the other, superior order rested on positive revealed norms (lex divina) acceptable only in faith and intelligible only to reason enlightened by faith. Both orders required authentic interpretation by the magisterium of the Church. This neo-scholastic theory of the magisterium is analogous in form to the medieval two-sword theory, analogous, that is, to Boniface VIII's imperial conception: ultimately the Church has authority over both. The Church's loss of direct political power and the associated recognition of the autonomy of politics brought with it a strengthening of the Church's authority over morality.

2. CRITICISMS OF REVEALED MORALITY

In reaction to the neo-scholastic dichotomy between reason and revelation, which in the end were linked only institutionallly, and also in reaction to the Enlightenment, efforts were made in the nineteenth century to increase the theological content of the concept of morality. In the twentieth century this development was reinforced. Its culmination was the derivation of a specific detailed ethics from the 'idea of the imitation of Christ' (F. Tillmann). Even today, however, the position that essential elements of Christian morality can only be securely established by recourse to theology is defended by important theologians (e.g. J. Ratzinger, H. Urs von Balthasar).

We cannot here go into the details of particular positions. Furthermore, there is no such thing as a single approach to 'revealed morality' or, as some prefer to say 'the ethics of faith'. At least three positions can be distinguished, the moral dogmatic, the biblicist and one based on orthopraxy.

The essential premiss of the moral dogmatic position is that Christian ethics contains infallible moral propositions, guaranteed with greater or lesser explicitness by the living tradition or revealed morality: the prohibition on the direct taking of innocent life, lifelong marital fidelity. These, it is argued, are truths for which human reason cannot in the end be a criterion because only reason enlightened by these truths could gain access to them. Consequently the appropriate means of establishing such moral dogmas is the continuity of tradition. (The exegesis of a period, we are reminded, is itself dependent on the ideas of the period.) In other words, the moral dogmatic position ties the core of Christian ethics to the competence of authority: 'Even today the Church cannot renounce this authority, and where it is in principle denied the competence to make detailed decisions for or against an intepretation of morality derived from grace the fundamental structure of the apostolic tradition is itself being shaken.'[3]

The moral dogmatic position thus coincides in its institutional implications with neo-scholasticism, even though it defines the relation between nature and grace in less dualistic terms. The same is true of another position in revealed morality, the biblicist position. Exegetes in particular rightly see the strong connection between any moral statement in scripture and theological statements. In the Bible the attitude to morality and the idea of God are intimately connected. The question is merely whether this connection is necessary for a better understanding of Christian ethics or also to justify the normative propositions of Christian ethics. The two are not distinguished by the biblicists, who accordingly regard the justification of particular normative propositions as a matter of the contemporary application of moral statements from scripture. If this application is to be preserved from arbitrariness, the only recourse is to authority.

The orthopraxy position, as it is found in political theologies, operates with a fundamental biblical criterion which it applies as a *norma normans* to Christian judgements and actions, the 'option for the poor'. Liberation theologians of course realise that this criterion alone is not sufficient to generate clear norms of action. This also means that it is not a criterion of justifying Christian ethics, but for the critical testing of the Christianity of Christian ethics. The proving of specific norms of action, on the other hand seems usually to be carried out by dialectical methods: norms are seen as 'practical negations' of evil reality. Recognition of wrong provokes the recognition of right. One problem with this position is that it does not examine the relationship between proof and critical testing and so leaves open the relationship between faith and reason in Christian morality. The problem with all positions based on revealed morality seems to me to be that, while they see the limits of reason and the danger of reducing the Gospel to the role of confirming current moral convictions, they have no refuge from the dependence of their own reason other than a retreat into authority or a headlong dash into eschatological criticism, neither of which is susceptible of rational testing.

Since in addition the use of scientific and philosophical procedures in argumentation is not subjected to scrutiny, there is a danger that positions based on revealed morality always have 'Trojan horses' within their walls. All varieties of this position, since they do not make explicit the philosophical ethics they must inevitably use if they seek to make normative statements, are constantly in danger of interpreting revelation to suit their needs. This problem appears in environmental ethics and peace ethics, where, for example, the divine injunctions about the created world or the eschatological reservation about all violence are 'applied' in quite different ways, according to the political or ethical statement at which it is desired to arrive.

I have quite often recently met young people who regard ethics as a matter of taking a stand and not a matter of discursive knowledge. For them a moral philosopher is a person who bears witness. While there are no objections to taking moral stands, the most important quality of any moral philosopher is nevertheless patience in argument. Not every Christian orthopractitioner may feel himself capable of this, but that is not a reason for treating it as unnecessary.

3. CRITICISMS OF AUTONOMOUS MORALITY

The 'autonomous morality' model came into being as a result of the recognition of the inadequacy both of the neo-scholastic model and of the 'revealed morality' model.

Another feature of it is that it gives particular emphasis to the problem of the authority of the *magisterium in rebus moralibus*. Within the framework of this model it makes sense to speak of humanness as a criterion of Christian existence.

It is precisely this that attracts the objections. How can humanness be a criterion of Christianity when it is Christianity which reveals 'true humanity' in faith in Christ? Is not the Englightenment's faith in reason, with its goal of the autonomy of ethics, in open competition with the Christian faith? And has not this very stress on moral autonomy since the Englightenment produced an ethical subjectivism and individualism which has negative effects in many areas of life, e.g. in the problems of sexual behaviour, divorce, birth control, abortion, euthanasia and suicide?

The objections lying behind these questions can be summarised in the following propositions. First, without the message of sin and redemption it is impossible to recognise the true dimensions of human dignity, and modern humanism accordingly offers an image of the human being reduced to the dimension of reason. Second, the autonomy of the subject in the modern period has led to the ideology of moral permissiveness without any standards. The 'autonomous morality' model is thus tainted with the charge of agnosticism and false liberalism. How is the unity of morality to be asserted without God and a guiding authority?

As the discussion of the last few years has shown, many of these objections rest on misunderstandings. As regards the charge of liberalism, autonomy is not the same as autarchy; a moral commitment to freedom and human dignity is not the same as a total absence of restraint. Autonomy is the absence of arbitrariness. It attempts to combine freedom and duty. A morality based on autonomy is under an obligation not to fall short of human dignity; or, as Kant puts it, a human being may never be merely a means; he or she must always be also the end of an action.[4] This is in no sense to deny that human beings are sinful and remain in need of redemption. Human reason as a criterion of morality also throws light on the limits of reason and so leaves room for the hope which faith can bring.

This in itself makes clear that the charge of agnosticism applies only where a connection between autonomous ethics and Christian hope is actively excluded in advance. It cannot be denied that this has constantly been done by followers of Fichte and Feuerbach. Strictly in terms of moral inquiry, however, agnosticism is not obligatory. The main feature of moral autonomy is simply a methodological separation of Kant's two questions, 'What should I do?' and 'What may I hope for?' The proof of moral obligation is methodologically independent of religious premises. On the other hand, it is clear that the ultimate interpretation of moral obligation leads into the question of faith, as it did for Kant.

But it is not enough to expose misunderstandings. It is also necessary to show what positive theological meaning the model of 'autonomous morality' can have. Part of this positive meaning lies in the traditional idea of 'natural morality' in the context of faith. According to Thomas Aquinas, moral rules are justified *secundum rationem*, and revelation does not have independent normative force which is exempt from this justification. This position avoids two problems, on the one hand the voluntarism of an ethics based on faith, which might seek to do without justification, and second a moralisation of faith on the ground that propositions of faith and propositions of morality were identical.

The central theological significance of 'autonomous morality', however, is that theology also holds that human freedom and dignity are the ultimate basis of the moral law. This is what we mean when we say in religious language that we want to glorify God and do his will. If we meant anything else we would be expressing a divine narcissism: God glorifies himself and uses us as an instrument. But God glorifies himself in the humanity of Jesus of Nazareth and he reveals his will as love for the perfected humanity of human beings. In order to give honour to God there is therefore no need to reduce human dignity. There is no competition between God and the humanity of man.

Nevertheless in a critical assessment of an 'autonomous morality' within a Christian context there is a remainder unaccounted for. 'Autonomous morality' provides a basis for a 'morality of autonomy', i.e. a morality which gives priority to human freedom and dignity. A Christian preference for a 'morality of autonomy' takes the form of a choice of the problem of 'freedom' as the basic criterion of ethics and the basic criterion of Christian existence.[5]

4. A MORALITY OF FREEDOM OR A MORALITY OF SOLIDARITY?

Is an ethos of autonomy compatible with an ethos based on Christianity? An initial reply might be that the Christian ethos too is an ethos of freedom: rules exist for human beings and not human beings for the sake of rules. This is attested by Jesus' attitude to the sabbath commandment, and Paul proclaims the freedom of the Gospel in contrast to the Law.

Nevertheless it is clear, for example in 1 Corinthians, that the call to freedom calls for responsibility towards one's neighbour. Freedom must build up the community and not destroy it. It must make itself dependent on the weak in love, and in the end it does not oppose God's freedom to do what he will with his servant. Because this is so, the Christian ethos is always better demonstrated by the criterion of love than by the criterion of freedom. Though Christians are no longer slaves, since they have been freed by God, a Christian ethos of autonomy cannot be an ethos of independence pure and simple. Where love rules, a person is in a relationship, in liberating dependence. Here again we need to draw attention to the contrast between autonomy (making one's own laws) and autarchy (having one's own way, sovereignty, absence of restraint). Not the clearly defined concept, but the term and idea of autonomy are to be found in Paul, in Romans' 'The Gentiles . . . are a law to themselves,' and the reason is that 'what the law requires is written on their hearts' (Rom. 2:15,15).[6] This makes clear that automony is simply concerned with the discovery and proving of moral rules, not with their free invention and subjective application. In the same way freedom and love are also not contradictory because love presupposes respect for the free structure of the other and freedom needs solidarity if it is to apply to more than one subject. (That is why human rights, for example, are bound up with solidarity.)

If freedom is shaped by the freedom of others, if love contains the idea of liberating others, then there is no real opposition between a morality of freedom and a morality of solidarity. There is then no contradiction between the ethos of Christian love and autonomous morality.

Nevertheless, despite this compatibility in principle it cannot be denied that the post-Christian development of modern humanism has in practice quite often interpreted autonomy as something like autarchy. This, however, makes obsolete not only a theological connection with ethics, but also an ethos of love. It is therefore easier for a Christian ethos of liberation, which understands freedom in terms of solidarity with the disadvantaged, to bring freedom and love into relation than an ethos of freedom which applies individual freedom to everyone. The dialectic of freedom and love in the Christian view must thus be envisaged in such a way that the entry point remains love.

5. IS THE GOSPEL NEUTRAL?

These ideas bring us staight back to the question about the Gospel. Does not the autonomy of ethics and the associated attitude of autonomy deprive the Gospel of practical efficacy, leave it on the level of good intentions and treat it as simply a decoration to moral propositions discovered by human beings and human reason? God blesses our free moral discoveries, since our power to make them comes from him. He does not compete with our moral freedom because his truth is given expression in it. But does that not mean that we fall into a deism in ethics and rob ethics of its inner religious passion? Or does it mean that there are two Christian attitudes, one shared with all people of good will and one consisting of a set of religious obligations which other people know nothing about and, simply to be moral, do not need to know about?

The 'sermon on the mount', of course, as a glance will show, is anything but neutral. On the other hand it is not interested in giving the maxims it proclaims any Christian exclusiveness. It does not base any maxims on a mystery of faith. What it does do is to give them a dimension of promise, which is in the strict sense theological, the beatitude. This feature, which makes the sermon on the mount and other Gospel maxims Christian, is *more* than morality.

I would single out five features as characteristic of the Gospel attitude. First, the important thing is not moral exclusiveness, but an unprecedented intensity in the maxims. Second, anyone who really wants to act morally well and correctly cannot stop at ethics but must go on to include the (religious) question of meaning, the question of the hope of our existence. Third, in the Christian view freedom and love cannot be separated, but the starting point is love. Fourth, the radical quality of the Gospel's ethical maxims is directed towards a catharsis of the mind which sees its salvation in the law. Fifth, in place of radical prescription of behaviour we have radical inspiration based on discipleship. The word does not become a moral law but a radical sign of practical commitment. An ethical system is replaced by the orthopraxy of faith.

Therefore it is quite right to say that the autonomy of ethics and the orthopraxy of faith constitute Christian morality. The autonomy of ethics accordingly does not neutralise the moral impulse of the Gospel but intensifies it. I can no longer say that what Jesus demands of us is ultimately a mystery of faith. I have to say that it has an ethical self-evidence.

The Gospel is not neutralised if the ethical maxims of justice are based on the idea of human dignity or can be provoked by the experience of the contrast in human suffering. The Gospel would be neutralised if it then retreated to what is its specific feature, the promise: place your hope in the promise in heaven. But the Gospel does not base its claim on exclusiveness, but on the intensity of its humanistic involvement. The Gospel relies on the identity (*indistinctio*) of ethical autonomy and believing orthopraxy, and thereby humanness as a criterion of Christian existence certainly becomes permissible, and even necessary. There can be no doubt that this has profound implications for the Church's moral teaching, for its pastoral work, political activity, its law codes and other practically oriented statements. It makes a fundamental difference to one's choice whether the criterion of an ethical method consists in the difference between Christian and non-Christian humanness or in the very lack of difference between them in relation to humanness as such. In the one case I would always look for an exclusive method, in the other for an inclusive method. In the one case humanistic opposition would not worry me, but encourage me, though it is no indication of a possibility of falsifying theological thinking. In the other case it is a *locus theologicus* which prompts us to re-examine the theology of ethics. Since deciding in favour of the absence of distinction between the human and the Christian in morality raises a profoundly theological question, we shall end with some reflections on its significance.

6. THEOLOGICAL REFLECTIONS ON THE LACK OF DISTINCTION (INDISTINCTIO) BETWEEN THE HUMAN AND THE CHRISTIAN[7]

The impossibility of distinguishing in ethics between what is human and what is Christian is by no means a ground for theological complaint. Theologically it is logical, both as regards the relationship between God and man in general and as regards the God-man relationship in Christology.

The divine and the human worlds cannot be distinguished like things of the same class. Normally when we make a distinction between two things we must have a third criterion by which we make the distinction, a quantity or a quality. God, however, does not come under our categorial criteria, and so the divine and human worlds are not only not separate; they are also, in the categorial sense, indistinguishable. Meister Eckhart, who took this idea the furthest, uses the example of the relation of one to the other numbers. The numbers come from one and are contained in one, but one transcends the category of multiplicity by which the other numbers are compared with each other. For our purposes it does not matter whether the example makes mathematical sense; what is important is the general point it is trying to illustrate about the God-man relationship.

From the point of view of categorial distinction, then, there is no distinction between the divine and the human. This is not to deny the difference; the point is that the quality of the distinction changes. It is no longer a categorial or a proportional distinction, but a relational one. It seems paradoxical when Eckhart says that it is a distinction by absence of distinction, but the difficulty is more linguistic than real. If one contains no distinctions (*unum est indistinctum*), this very lack of distinction distinguishes it from things which are categorially distinguished. If we apply this to Christian ethics, the very fact that Christianity makes no claim to a special religious ethics, it has a specific relationship, arising out of faith, to ethics in general: God accepts human beings without reservation. Seen in this way, it is not surprising that autonomous ethics grew up in the Christian West.

This can be confirmed and developed by a Christological consideration. The two natures in Christ, tradition says, can be distinguished. Their identity is a personal one. The distinction between them, however, is not categorial, as though divine 'nature' and human 'nature' were things of the same order. Here too the distinction is relational, and must be treated categorially as an absence of distinction. Here again the purpose of distinction between divine and human is not rejected; it is simply transposed into the proper dimension.

The relationship between Christian and human ethics is similar. If a categorial distinction between them were possible, the Christian faith would no longer be a relationship to ethics, but simply a type of ethics, and this is a view Christianity specifically rejects in the 'Gospel and law' argument. We have good grounds for treating the relationship of the Christian and the human as relational. But that means that Christian faith is a crucial context for Christian ethics; it is not Christian ethics as such. Being a context for ethics means that the Christian faith opts for a particular human ethics which deserves that title, an ethics of autonomy and solidarity. In other words, the distinctive feature of the relationship between the orthopraxy of faith and the autonomy of ethics is their indistinguishability in practice.

This consideration demonstrates not only why the moral thrust of the Gospel is not reduced by an approach based on the autonomy of ethics; it also makes clear the extent to which the human can be regarded as a criterion of the Christian. Adapting the scholastic axiom about nature and grace, we could say that faith presupposes the idea of achieved humanity, and exalts and perfects this idea. Note that in this formula faith is the subject of this dynamic. Faith starts from the premiss—in morals as elsewhere—that everything in encompassed in advance by God's grace. Created existence too is existence, not by one's own resources, but *ab alio*; it is received existence, dependent existence.

In this way the relation 'faith' constitutes the wider context for the ethical text. The ethical concepts of failure and the new start are thus placed in the context of human failure and Christian reconciliation. This also removes the ethical optimism of the progressive redemption of human beings by morality and frees us to hope in a God who has more than moral criteria.

7. CONCLUDING REMARK: PROVING AND UNDERSTANDING

It is a premiss of autonomous morality that moral norms do not require the authority of theological propositions to be provable by reason. If this were so, we should constantly be forced to make propositions of faith plausible before we could prove propositions of ethics. It is part of the Christian tradition that the Gospel is not required to prove the validity of ethical propositions. And the fact that the Gospel is concerned with more than ethics is similarly obvious.

And yet what happens when the context of faith interprets the ethical text? Evidently, as we have seen, the attitude to ethics and the way it is used change. On the one hand, human ethical choices acquire unprecedented importance, since the Christian's salvation is decided by love of neighbour (see Matt. 25). On the other hand, Christian use of ethics is not directed to the imposition of discipline on the community or morality on the world at large, but to liberation. The prime element in the attitude of the 'sermon on the mount' is the beatitudes. Ethics too is not meant to judge, but to save.

It seems to me that the Gospel's final contribution to ethics consists in interpreting ethics in terms of hope. As a humanist agnostic, all one can say in the end is, 'Even without hope for the suffering humanity of the past, the present or the future, I can do nothing other than follow the logic of responsibility.' This is the course adopted by Albert Camus' Dr D. Rieux in *The Plague*. Judged by criteria of efficacy, ethical commitment often seems absurd; it is like a tiny flickering flame in a darkened world. But the Gospel tells us that God takes responsibility for efficacy, and gives the whole world a share in the little we contribute. Because through faith we have reason for real hope, we understand the meaning of obligation. This means that we can not only prove ethical propositions, but can also understand their underlying meaning. Because this meaning concerns us inescapably, it removes any possibility of our remaining neutral towards the demands of ethics.

Translated by Francis McDonagh

Notes

1. See the theological discussion on the autonomy of ethics: A. Auer *Autonome Moral und christlicher Glaube* (Düsseldorf 1971); *Ethik im Kontext des Glaubens* ed. D. Mieth and F. Compagnoni (Freiburg 1978); *Autonomie, Dimensions éthiques de la liberté* ed. C. J. Pinto de Oliveira (Fribourg & Paris 1979); *Anspruch der Wirklichkeit und christlicher Glaube* ed. D. Mieth and H. Weber (Düsseldorf 1980); K. W. Merks *Theologische Grundlegung der sittlichen Autonomie* (Düsseldorf 1979).

2. See J. Ratzinger *Prinzipien christlicher Moral* (Einsiedeln 1975) p. 43ff.

3. J. Ratzinger *ibid.* p. 66.

4. See Kant *Grundlegung zur Metaphysik der Sitten,* Akademie-Ausgabe (Berlin 1903), IV, p. 428.

5. On this and the next section, see H. Frings 'Freiheit, ein Versuch, Gott zu denken' *Philos. Jahrbuch* 77 (1970) 225-237; *id.*, 'Gott' *Handbuch Philosophischer Grundbegriffe* 3 (Munich 1973) pp. 629-641.

6. See R. Hasenstab *Modelle paulinischer Ethik, Beiträge zu einem Autonomie-Modell aus paulinischem Geist* (Mainz 1977).

7. The ideas which follow are stimulated by Meister Eckhart. See esp. *Die lateinischen Werke* (Stuttgart 1954) II pp. 109ff and 482ff, and H. Fischer *Meister Eckhart* (Munich 1974) pp. 124-129.

D

Norbert Greinacher

Human Rights and Christian Rights

1. INTRODUCTION

IN AN issue devoted to the relationship between the 'human' and the 'Christian', humanity and Christianity, we cannot omit a discussion of the relationship between human rights and our rights as Christians. The question of 'Christian rights' is a critical instance, throwing into relief the fundamental problem in a particular concrete form; an examination of this one instance will shed light, in all probability, on the wider question.

People have discussed the question of human rights for hundreds of years, but in the last few decades a consensus seems to have crystallised with regard to the central areas of human rights. This basic consensus found expression primarily in the United Nations 'General Declaration of Human Rights of 10 December 1948' and in the 'United Nations Human Rights Convention of 16 December 1966'.

The idea of 'Christian rights', however, is relatively new. To my knowledge it was used for the first time in the 'Founding Declaration of the Committee for the Defence of Christian rights in the Church of 19 December 1979'. This Committee was formed in the Federal German Republic as a response to the withdrawal of Hans Küng's authority to teach.[1] The declaration runs as follows:

> 'The rights of Christians in the Church are being threatened. It is becoming more and more evident that the Church's leadership is characterised by arbitrary acts, violations of fundamental rights and authoritarian decisions. There is an attempt to enforce a particular understanding of the truth at the expense of the happiness of millions. This is in clear contradiction of the liberating Gospel of Jesus Christ, a Gospel which breaks through all barriers.
>
> We are appalled to see such an opposton between these inquisitorial measures and the command of Jesus—love and reconciliation. While the Church cannot do without its official proclamation, this proclamation must minister to the Gospel of Jesus Christ and the faith of men and women; it is not for the bolstering up of an elite.
>
> We affirm the following:
> Instead of setting an example by implementing as Christian rights the basic rights of every human being as achieved by the French Revolution—and to do so would accord with the Church's mission—the Church today, though it often proclaims these rights, is far from promoting them in its own ambit.

40

Consequently we demand:

—that the Church shall not fall behind in respecting the fundamental democratic rights of all men and women won as a result of the Enlightenment; in particular that it shall not obstruct freedom of thought and conscience, nor inflict punishment on critical thinkers, nor tolerate trials or hearings in which those prosecuting have all the rights and the accused have as good as none, nor promote dependent relationships based on authority, punishment and obedience rather than on collegiality and brotherhood, nor offend against the laws of tolerance and mutual respect'[1].

But the question is, does the Christian have rights? 'Can a case be made at all? Is it not the height of presumption to be making claims of any sort when approaching the altar? Surely the only proper attitude here is humility?[2] And against whom is the Christian going to vindicate his rights? Against God, his fellow Christians, Church authorities or institutions? Does the maxim not apply here: No law, no plaintiff? For to what law can the Christian appeal? The Codex Juris Canonici, which scarcely even refers to those not ordained? To what authority can he appeal for his rights as a Christian? *Are* these rights with a determinate 'Christian' content? And if so, what is their relation to human rights? Is it not better to speak of 'human rights within the Church'?[3]

This is by no means all. It is not humbug to speak of Christian rights when we consider the way the two major Christian bodies have acted in the past and still do act? Surely these rights are a dead letter if, as is the case in certain diaconal training centres in the Evangelical Church, women who have been newly instituted are asked at the end of their probationary period whether they are pregnant—and, if they say Yes, are not employed further? Where are 'Christian rights' when those who are divorced and remarried are refused communion in the Catholic Church? What has happened to the 'freedom of the Christian', in Luther's phrase, when an Evangelical woman theologian is barred from promotion because her husband is a Catholic theologian? And what about the freedom of theological research, especially in the Catholic Church? The situation is bleak enough. All of us have our own experience of the practice of both Christian churches, a practice which, from the point of view of freedom, has been a tale of woe.

2. THE BIBLICAL TRADITION: A LIBERATING MESSAGE OF GOOD WILL TOWARDS MEN

First, however, let us see what perspectives arise out of the Judeo-Christian tradition with regard to human rights and Christian rights.[4]

Our *raison d'être* for discussing, promoting and campaigning for human rights depends on how we view the human being; it depends on the current concept of man. The broader and more convincing our rationale of human dignity, the more evident are human rights and the more urgent is the task of implementing them.

What follows is a sketch of a Christian and theological foundation for human rights. This does not imply a low opinion of other approaches—the Stoics, for example, or modern atheistic humanism—but takes them for granted. Put another way: in the past and present non-Christians have shown that they can provide a convincing rationale of human rights, and have often done more than Christians to put them into practice. Here I merely propose the thesis that on the basis of the Judeo-Christian tradition the human being gains in specific importance, i.e., that human dignity (and thus human rights) can be justified in an even more convincing and exigent manner.

The foundation of this kind of theological rationale must be the fact that the human being is made in the image of God. In the myths of many peoples the king alone is regarded as God's likeness on earth. 'The Prince is the shadow of God, and the people are the shadow of the Prince'—so runs a Babylonian treatise on statecraft.[5] In contrast we read in Genesis 1:27; 'God made man in his own image, in the image of God he created him; male and female he created them.' Whatever be the meaning of mankind's 'likeness' to God, it is clear that human dignity and the rights arising from it are emphasised here in an unsurpassable way. From this vantage-point any affront to human dignity and rights is no longer only a trespass against one's fellow men, but blasphemy, a challenge to God himself.[6]

Jesus of Nazareth built on this Old Testament foundation; indeed, he traced the features of human dignity even more clearly. What he says concerning men and women, backed up by his own example in action, actually applies to all people, but in a special way it applies to those who commit themselves to his person and cause. Thus he gives to Christians an encompassing, inalienable dignity, in turn yielding Christian rights.

In his life and teaching Jesus of Nazareth bore witness to the fact that the reality which enfolds all things is a benevolent God; in doing so he removed man's anxiety with regard to God. He freed the Hellenistic-Roman world from the fear of fate, whether as dependence on the gods or on the sway of the stars. At the same time he destroyed the power of the Jewish clerical class to use 'God' as an instrument of terror. Henceforward it is impossible to cite Jesus of Nazareth when using 'God' to induce anxiety in others.

By witnessing to and living out the maternal and fatherly love of God, and true brotherly and sisterly love, Jesus demands the fundamental equality of all men and women. Paul was later to formulate it thus: 'There is neither Jew nor Greek, there is neither slave nor free, there is neither male nor female; for you are all one in Christ Jesus' (Gal. 3:28).

God has revealed himself in Jesus as the one who accepts all men and women, completely and irrevocably. He has affirmed mankind. As a result of this, every person receives a dignity which no one else can give him, and which no one can take from him.

At the centre of the preaching of Jesus stands the reality of the reign of God; this demolishes the justification for any kind of reign of dominion of man over man. It also prevents us idolising or making absolute any political power or infrahistorical entity, whether a *Führer*, a particular race, class, sex or nation.

Jesus saw that his central mission was to be available 'for us men and for our salvation' and thus expressed the identity of mankind's search for happiness and well-being and the concern of God for man. This invalidates all heteronomy and alienation with regard to man. God does not want man's self-renunciation; he is happy when man is happy. 'What is specific to the biblical message is that the God of Israel, the God of the prophets and Jesus himself enters the field on behalf of man's right; 'through grace', i.e., in sovereign freedom and love, in his 'endless mercy and compassion' for man down-trodden and exploited, he proclaims the latter's right as a human being. Here God himself appears as the ultimate guarantor of man's inalienable, absolute right to life and existence.'[7]

Since Jesus Christ is the only mediator between God and man (see 1 Tim. 2:5), Christians are no longer under the tutelage of mediatorial sacral institutions. They are subject neither to the supremacy of law of the Old Covenant, nor to any personal or institutional mediators. In the New Covenant, Christians receive a free, direct relationship with God and his saving activity.

In particular, Jesus took up the cause of those deprived of basic freedoms—women, children, the sick, tax-collectors, prostitutes and aliens—and thus he made a more radical demand for the recognition of the rights of everyman. There is little danger in maintaining the dignity of the privileged; but it is a deadly serious matter to be seen to support those whose human dignity is being trampled on.

Those who have become involved with Jesus he no longer calls servants but friends (see John 15:15)—thus he emancipates Christians. 'So through God you are no longer a slave but a son, and if a son then an heir' (Gal. 4:7). Formerly objects of alien domination, now they are subjects of their own lives and their own history.[8]

Paul continues this tradition. To the Galatians he writes: 'For freedom Christ has set us free; stand fast therefore, and do not submit again to a yoke of slavery' (5:1). What else does the Pauline doctrine of justification mean but that God justifies man, makes him righteous, freely, 'gratis', without any achievement on man's side, and reconciles him with his fellow men and with himself? In this way he acquires a right and a rank in the presence of God. Thus in Romans: 'If God is for us, who is against us? He who did not spare his own Son but gave him up for us all, will he not also give us all things with him? Who shall bring any charge against God's elect? It is God who justifies; who is to condemn? Is it Christ Jesus, who died, yes, who was raised from the dead, who is at the right hand of God, who indeed intercedes for us? Who shall separate us from the love of Christ?' (8:31-35).

With regard to this Pauline doctrine of justification Josef Blank rightly says: 'The whole Church with all its members—without any hierarchical exceptions—is subject to this "fundamental right" or "dignity" . . . This can be described as the theological basis of Christian rights and of canon law.'[9]

3. VICISSITUDES IN THE HISTORY OF THIS LIBERATING MESSAGE

What has happened to this liberating message of the New Testament in almost two thousand years of Christian history? Ernst Käsemann states that 'the struggle to vindicate the vocation of freedom goes right through the history of the Church.' He continues: 'It must be taken up anew in every generation and in the life of every Christian.'[10]

Within the compass of this paper we cannot give even the roughest historical outline of the effect on the world of Jesus of Nazareth's liberating, beneficent Gospel. But, at the risk of oversimplifying, let us indicate two distinctive tendencies.

The attempt to put into practice the human dignity proclaimed by Jesus Christ, and the human rights arising from it, has never slackened in the Church. Again and again individuals, groups, and even whole movements have arisen, taking seriously—as seriously as Jesus himself the reality of human freedom as documented in Jesus. They did not work to bring about this fundamental freedom of the human being only within the Church; they knew that freedom cannot be compartmentalised and must be brought about, for the sake of human beings, outside the immediate area of the Church as well as inside.

Ambrose opposed the Emperor Theodosius to his face when the latter had created a bloodbath in Thessalonika. Bartholomew de las Casas vehemently protested to the Spanish King about the genocide of Indians in Latin America. And when tracing the Christian line on the issue of freedom we should not be preoccupied with the actions of Church officers. For the spirit of Christian freedom blows (and blows today) also among the so-called simple Church members, among the Church's marginalised groups, among excluded heretics and sects, in the Free churches and in charismatic groups. Today many Christians, and even whole national churches in the Third and Fourth World, are inspired by the theology of liberation and involved in the struggle for the rights of the oppressed; this is an expression of the inherited Christian concern for freedom.

Yet, to be honest, one must admit that another tendency has been more influential in the history of Christianity, namely, the fight of the institutionalised Christian churches against all efforts and movements designed to achieve freedom, both within the Church and outside it. Surely Ernst Käsemann is right when he judges that 'in this sense, the history of Christian freedom is a way of sorrows on which the churches must look back with shame rather than pride.'[11]

There have been terrible perversions of the Christian message: the fateful axiom 'outside the Church no salvation' with its dire consequences for millions of people; the way the invitation offered by the Good News was replaced by a compulsion: *'compelle intrare*—compel them to come in'; the heretical statements of Pope Boniface VIII's Bull 'Unam sanctum' with its absolute claims regarding the Church; the Inquisition with its burning of heretics and witches; the cases of Luther and Galileo; the baneful conclusion of the Rites Controversy in the Indian and China missions in the seventeenth and eighteenth centuries; all this and more represents a betrayal of the liberating message of the New Testament.

Furthermore it has been very unfortunate that Christian freedom in the Church has too often been spiritualised and relegated to the realm of interiority. In one respect Herbert Marcus is only too accurate when he writes: 'Since the Reformation a particular concept of freedom has dominated bourgeois theory, namely, the union of internal autonomy and external heteronomy, the regeneration of freedom with bondage as a result of its abuse . . . Christian teaching on freedom pushes man's "liberation" into the past, before his actual history begins. His history is then the history of his bondage, an "eternal" consequence of his "liberation". In Christianity, strictly speaking, there is no historical liberation for men and women; or rather, any such liberation has primarily a negative value, namely, the partial liberation from God, becoming free to do evil—symbolised in the Fall.'[12]

4. CHRISTIANITY AND THE GROWTH OF HUMAN RIGHTS

The influence of Christianity on the development and implementation of classical human rights (conceived individualistically) is disputed. Cautiously, however, we may advance two observations.

First it is clear that certain central affirmations of Christian faith are very closely related to human rights. The history of freedom in modern times, with its emancipation movements, is unthinkable, both in its origins and in its actual course, without the influence of the Christian idea of freedom.[13] This is not to say that it is the only source. But at the time of the French Revolution, for instance, significant contributions were made by the lower clergy in Paris; thus it was not an accident that the basic Christian values of liberty, equality and fraternity became the Revolution's watchword.[14] Hegel is right when he says, in his *Lectures on the Philosophy of History*, 'that the orientals only knew that *one* person was free, whereas the Greek and Roman world knew that a certain number were free; we, however, know that all men and women are free *per se*; i.e., they are free because they are human beings.'[15]

Secondly, however, we must add that in the eighteenth and nineteenth centuries the human rights of individuals in the political sphere were implemented against the bitter opposition of the Christian churches, pre-eminently the Catholic Church. Thus, for instance, looking back at the French declaration of the riots of men and citizens of 1789, Pope Pius VI writes in his Brief 'Quod aliquantum' (10.3.1791): 'The National Assembly sang the praises of this equality and liberty; but where did it lead? Only to the overthrow of the Catholic religion. Consequently the Assembly refused to pronounce the latter to be the dominant religion of the Kingdom, although this had always been the Church's due title.' He expressed similar sentiments in the Brief 'Caritas' (13.4.1791). Then there was the Encyclical of Pope Gregory XVI 'Mirari vos arbitramur' (15.8.1832), which castigated freedom of consequence as a 'false opinion, indeed madness' or the Encyclical 'Quanta cura' and the 'Syllabus' of Pope Pius X (8.12.1864). It was not until the Encyclical 'Pacem in terris' of Pope John XXIII (11.4.1963) and the 'Pastoral Constitution on the Church in the Modern World' of Vatican II that a change at last came about in the attitude towards individual human rights.

There is, however, a further issue. As developed gradually in the West, the form and content of human rights suffer from a certain historically understandable bias and from certain deficiencies. It was characteristic of the constitutions of the European states and of North America to be particularly concerned with the human rights of *individuals*; this was the political side of the economic emancipation of the middle class and its legal safeguard. The constitution was primarily to protect the proprietory citizen against the state. Typically, for instance, in the French declaration of human rights of 1791 the right to property immediately follws the right to freedom. It is therefore correct to speak of a 'proprietory individualism'.[17]

Right from the outset, in spite of the commitment to liberty and equality for all, this means that some people are still 'more equal than others'—there are those with property, and those to whom the right to property means little because they have none. 'Human rights' were made to underwrite the existing order and the new economic power structures; but the latter were inevitably in complete opposition to the fuller development of human rights. This concept of 'human rights' had become an ideology legitimising the propertied middle class, which could successfully defend its own privileges under the pretext of campaigning for the human rights of individuals. Karl Marx saw this clearly: 'The practical use to which the human right of freedom is put is the right to private property . . . That is, the right to enjoy and dispose of one's wealth without reference to others, independently of society; the right of self-interest. This individualistic freedom and the use to which it is put form the basis of bourgeois society. It causes every man to see in his neighbour not the fulfilment, but the restriction, of his freedom.'[18] To this very day, the task of prosecuting human rights for all suffers from this same dilemma.

Since the Second World War the churches of the 'First World' have gradually recognised the importance of the human rights of individuals and their implications for Christianity; they became strong protagonists of these rights, and in doing so often gave them an additional religious charge. One of the factors at work here is the churches' (legitimate) interest in the matter; there is much reason to highlight freedom of religion and freedom of conscience under the heading of the rights of the individual. By doing this, however, the churches of the First World are willy-nilly in great danger of giving religious sanction to the existing national and international capitalist economic order, with all its injustices.

It is exceptionally urgent, therefore, to complement the classical and individualistic form of human rights with social rights such as were expressed in the 1966 'Human Rights Convention of the United Nations'. This has two parts: part A is the 'International Pact concerning Economic, Social and Cultural Rights' and part B is the 'International Pact concerning the Political Rights of Citizens'. It is to be regretted that this long-overdue complement was not pioneered by the Christian churches but by the 'children of this world'. Here, as in the fight for the right of individuals, they were more Christian than the churches. From the New Testament there can be no doubt that human rights conceived individualistically simply cry out for their social complement.[19]

5. THE RELATIONSHIP BETWEEN HUMAN RIGHTS AND CHRISTIAN RIGHTS

If, on the basis of the foregoing, we ask whether there *are* 'Christian rights' and, if so, how they are related to human rights, we discover both similarities and differences.

First of all: general human rights are Christian rights as well. For everything that is human is also Christian; everything that benefits the dignity and freedom of all men and women naturally applies to Christians.

The Christian will not limit God's activity in history to the Church alone, but sees

God at work even in the most human traditions of modern freedom. Walter Dirks is surely right in saying: 'The discovery of human rights among the peoples of Europe (and thence throughout the whole world) is a huge advance in the process of mankind's emancipation and maturity. It is one of the irreversible great events in which we must recognise God at work.'[20] Human rights as they have evolved in the West are also a belated result of the liberating message of Jesus of Nazareth. The tragedy of modern times is that the Church's officers have not recognised how much genuine Christianity has found expression in human rights. By condemning them they betrayed fundamental elements of the mission of Jesus himself. One can only underline the words of Walter Dirks: 'In the preface to the "Constitution on the Church in the Modern World" the Council affirmed that "The joy and hope, the grief and anguish of the men of our time . . . are the joy and hope, the grief and anguish of the followers of Christ as well." This implied that the great bourgeois revolution, at its best, and with its most profound consequences, seen as a step forward in the history of mankind's humanisation, is a constituent element of the pilgrim Church.'[21]

But quite apart from this broad convergence of general human rights and Christian rights, specific *Christian* rights arise out of the liberating Gospel of the New Testament, with regard to Church members. One has to regret that, typically, little thought has been given to this subject. The following is an attempt—by way of example and without further elaboration—to formulate some of these Christian rights; some of them arise automatically from general human rights, but, because of the current situation in both major Churches, need to be emphasised specially.[22]

—Every Christian, by virtue of baptism, has a right to belong to the Church.

—All Christians, irrespective of differences arising from their functions in the Church, have the same rights and obligations.

—Every Christian has the right to freedom of conscience.

—Every Christian has the right to live according to his own convictions on the basis of the Christian faith.

—Every Christian has the right to make his own political decisions and act on them, provided this does not directly contradict Christian faith.

—Every Christian has the right to witness to his Christian faith in his own cultural form.

—Every Christian has the right to research freely in the field of theology.

—Every Christian has the right and obligation to criticise Church officers and their decisions if he comes to the conclusion that their attitude is contrary to the spirit of the Christian Gospel.

—Christians have the right to form new groups of Christians or new Christian communities.

—Christian communities have the right to celebrate the eucharist regularly. Consequently they have a right to an ordained community leader.

—Every Christian has the right to Word and Sacrament, i.e., the right to hear the proclamation of the Christian message and to unhindered access to the sacraments.

—Every Christian has the right to advice and help from those who exercise the relevant ministries in the Church.

—Every Christian has a right to marriage.

—Every Christian has a right to be informed about all church matters.

—Every Christian has a right to active participation in worship.

—Every Christian has the right to develop his own spirituality.

—Every Christian has the right of appeal to superior authority against disciplinary decisions of a church officer or committee, and against verdicts in canon law.

—Every Christian has a right to participate in the choice of those church officers whose actions particularly concern him.

The author is aware of the fragmentary nature of these Christian rights. There are problems involved in substantiating them, in setting due limits and in avoiding misunderstandings in their formulation. But it is important to show that there *are* rights which are specifically 'Christian' by virtue of their concept, and that they urgently need thought and definition.

6. WORLDWIDE EFFORTS TOWARDS CHRISTIAN RIGHTS

It is astonishing how, in recent years, initiatives have been taken quite independently of one another in individual national churches to protect the rights of Christians. The 'Association for the Rights of Catholics in the Church' was founded in the U.S.A. in March 1980 with the aim of bringing about a considerable structural change in the Catholic Church. This association drew up a sketch of a 'Charter of Rights for Catholics in the Church'.[23] At Pentecost 1981 in France a committee was formed entitled 'Droits et libertés dans les Églises';[24] it appealed to all the Christians of France to support the drawing up of a Charter of Rights in the Catholic Church. Similar moves were made in Switzerland, Austria, Poland and the Federal German Republic.[25] In the F.G.R. the 'Committee for the Defence of Christian Rights in the Church' was founded on 19 December 1979. On 2 May 1981 spokespersons drafed the committee's role and aim in these terms:

1. The Committee sees itself as a movement within the Church composed of Christians who are members of their own Churches.
2. The Committee brings together members chiefly from the two major Christian Churches. Together they bear responsibility for implementing Christian rights in both Churches.
3. The members of the Committee are opposed to any and every form of domination by man over man. However, they recognise that form of Church authority which serves mankind in the spirit of Jesus Christ. They are ready to collaborate with Church officers.
4. The members of the Committee are working for an atmosphere of freedom in the Church, maturity of Church members, a public and critical frankness in the Church, and the solution of conflicts in a spirit of freedom.
5. The members of the Committee are opposed to the widespread sense of resignation in the Church. They not only look for liberating moves from Church officers; they are endeavouring step by step to cultivate freedom among themselves, in their own Church communities and through necessary discussions with the whole Church.
6. The committee tries to show solidarity with individual Church members or particular groups who have been specially affected by oppressive ecclesiastical measures. The Committee tries to help such people according to its resources and to act as an intermediary in existing conflicts.
7. In addition the Committee endeavours to deal with infringements of the rights of Christians by engaging in studies in the fields of law and theology.
8. The Committee wishes to concern itself primarily with the following problems: the situation of women in the Church; admission of those divorced and remarried to the sacraments; homosexuals in the Church; Church employees; laicised priests in the Catholic Church; Christians whose official permit to teach has been withdrawn, or who are being intimidated in their theological teaching and research.

These efforts are aimed at providing a comprehensive theological foundation and exposition of Christian rights; is it presumptuous to see in this movement a 'sign of the times'?

7. CHRISTIAN RIGHTS AND CANON LAW

If it is true that 'For freedom Christ has set us free' (Gal. 5:1), no one can deprive

Christians of their rights to freedom. They are given by Christ; every Christian has the right to exercise them. To an increasing degree, Christians will be free to speak and live in the Church according to this law of liberty. They are free to the extent that they enjoy their liberties and do not allow others to deprive them of them.

A great disappointment awaits us, however, if we compare this Christian rights movement with the 1976 draft of the 'Lex fundamentalis ecclesiae'[26] and the 'Schema Codicis Juris Canonici'[27]. At the time of writing the final text of both documents is not available, but the drafts published so far give rise to the gravest misgivings.

Every theological affirmation of the Church as the People of God has been completely eliminated. In its place the idea of the Church as a 'societas perfecta' has once more reared its head. One could have wished the Church's basic constitution to have sprung from these two principles:

'The freedom of those who believe in Christ—for which Christ has set them free—is promoted and protected by the Church to the highest possible degree. Since the Holy Spirit—who is the New Law—dwells in them, the purpose of the Church's legal prescriptions is to serve this law by defining and ratifying its demands.'

'The offices which exist in the Church are bound to work together for the welfare of the Church in such a way that the higher authority only acts in place of the lower if the latter is unable to achieve the goal in view.'[28]

On the contrary, the Church's draft constituion means that episcopal collegiality is practically liquidated; the document is marked by a deep distrust of lay involvement, and the desire to deprive the laity of any fundamental right to participate in the Church's leadership. Herwi Rikhof comes to the following conclusion: 'So laypeople's area of responsibility lies outside the Church; the highest rank open to them is to be co-operators with the hierarchy. Our general conclusion must be, therefore, that the 'Lex fundamentalis ecclesiae' and the 'Schema Codicis Juris Canonici' represent a step backwards. They are much more, then, than a mere missed opportunity.'[29]

From this it is clear that, far from setting an example by guaranteeing human and Christian rights, the new canon law is far behind human rights as they are formulated in the United Nations documents.

8. CONCLUSION

This is all the more frightening since the Church's credibility in modern society depends largely on whether it implements basic human rights within its own ambit. Its efforts for human rights and justice in society stand or fall on this issue. Thus the 1971 Synod of Bishops: 'In bearing witness to justice the Church is well aware that he who claims to speak to men about justice must first be seen to be just.'[30]

And in the message of the 1974 Synod of Bishops on 'Human rights and reconciliation' we read: 'The Church knows from experience that in order to minister to the spread of human rights in the world it is bound constantly to examine its conscience and ceaselessly to purify its own life, its legislation, its institutions and its modes of activity . . . Consequently we need to examine what relationships can be maintained with social systems and structures which encourage the infringement of human rights. Such encouragement should be publicly exposed.'[31] Finally we read this in a study by a Papal Commission for Justice and Peace entitled 'The Church and Human Rights' (1974): 'If its evangelical mission is to be effective, the Church must first of all put itself on the side of the rights of the human person, that they may be recognised, guaranteed, protected and extended in the world. Here it must begin by self-examination, taking a critical look at the extent to which these fundamental rights are assured and put into practice in its own organisation.'[32] What more can be said?

Translated by Graham Harrison

Notes

1. *Freiheitsrechte für Christen?* Warum die Kirche ein Grundgesetz braucht, ed. N. Greinacher-I. Jens (Munich 1980) p. 39f.
2. Walter Dirks raises these questions in the above book, p. 11.
3. See J. Neumann *Menschenrechte auch in der Kirche?* (Zurich 1976); *Menschenrechte in der Kirche* ed. M. Pilters-K. Walf (Düsseldorf 1980); 'The Church and the Rights of Man' in *Concilium* 124 (1979).
4. See chiefly: J. Blank 'The Justice of God as the Humanisation of Man—The Problem of Human Rights in the New Testament' *Concilium* 124 (1979) 27-38; 'Zur theologischen Begründung von "Christenrechte" ' in *Freiheitsrechte für Christen?* ed. N. Greinacher-I. Jens pp. 28-38; *Das Evangelium als Garantie der Freiheit* (Würzburg 1970); Huber-E. Tödt *Menschenrechte. Perspektiven einer menschlichen Welt* (Stuttgart 1977); E. Käsemann *Der Ruf der Freiheit* (Tübingen 1968); J Moltmann *Menschenwürde, Recht und Freiheit* (Stuttgart 1979); *Gottes Recht und Menschenrechte. Studien und Empfehlungen des reformierten Weltbundes* ed. J. M. Lochmann-J. Moltmann (Neukirchen 1977).
5. Quoted in J. Moltmann *Menschenwürde, Recht und Freiheit* p. 21.
6. On the Old Testament foundation for human rights: J. Limburg 'Human Rights in the Old Testament' in *Concilium* 124 (1979) 20 26.
7. J. Blank 'Zur theologischen Begründung von "Christenrechten" in *Freiheitsrechte für Christen?* ed. N. Greinacher-I. Jens p. 30f.
8. See J. B. Metz *Glaube in Geschichte und Gesellschaft* (Mainz 1977).
9. J. Blank 'Zur theologischen Begründung von "Christenrechten" ' p. 31.
10. E. Käsemann *Der Ruf der Freiheit* p. 8.
11. *Ibid.* p. 54.
12. *Ideen zu einer kritischen Theorie der Gesellschaft* (Frankfurt 1970) pp. 55-57.
13. See chiefly P. Plongeron 'Anathema or Dialogue? Christian Reactions to Declarations of the Rights of Man in the United States and Europe in the Eighteenth Century' in *Concilium* 124 (1979) 39-48.
14. H. Maier *Revolution and Kirche* (Freiburg 1965).
15. *Werke 12* (Frankfurt 1973) p. 32.
16. *Denzinger-Schönmetzer* 2730.
17. C. B. Macpherson *Die politische Theorie des Besitzindividualismus* (Frankfurt 1973).
18. *Zur Judenfrage:* Karl Marx—Friedrich Engels *Werke 1* (Berlin 1974) pp. 347-377; this reference p. 364f.
19. See N. Greinacher 'The Responsibility of the Churches in the First World for Establishing Human Rights' in *Concilium* 124 (1979) 107-115.
20. 'Menschen und Christenrechte in der Kirche' in *Freiheitsrechte für Christen?* ed. N. Greinacher-I. Jens p. 10.
21. *Ibid.* p. 10f.
22. See *Manifeste de la liberté chrétienne* (Paris 1975); 'Charter of the Rights of Catholics in the Church' in *Concilium* 147 (1981) 91f; 'Rechte und Rechtswege in der Kirche' in *Orientierung 45* (15/31.7.1981) 160-163.
23. See 'The Charter of the Rights of Catholics in the Church' *ibid*; (Association for the Rights of Catholics in the Church, c/o L. Swidler, Temple University, Philadelphia, Pennsylvania 191222, U.S.A.) For this and the next note, see *Freiheitsrechte in der Kirche?* ed. N. Greinacher-I. Jens pp. 39-79.
24. c/o 14, Rue Saint-Benoit, F-75006 Paris.
25. Switzerland: Verein zur Förderung der Vereinigung für die Anliegen von Konzil und Synode, Färberstr. 33, CH-8008 Zürich; Austria: A. Weiss, Eisteichgasse 25, A-8010 Graz; Poland: Groups of the common way; Federal German Republic: Anne Jensen, Charlottenstr. 21, D-7400 Tübingen.

26. *Herder-Korrespondenz* 32 (1978) pp. 617-632.

27. See 'The Revised Code of Canon Law: A Missed Opportunity' in *Concilium* 147 (1981).

28. Alberto Abelli 'Ein Grundgesetz der Restauration' in *Herder-Korrespondenz* 33 (1979) pp. 36-43, this reference p. 38f.

29. *Concilium* 147 (1981) p. 63.

30. *Herder-Korrespondenz* 26 (1972) p. 37.

31. *Herder-Korrespondenz* 28 (1974) p. 625.

32. *Die Kirche und die Menschenrechte. Ein Arbeitspapier der Päpstlichen Kommission Justitia et Pax* (Munich 1976) no. 62. p. 28f.

Xavier Thévenot

Christianity and Sexual Fulfilment

'WHOEVER FOLLOWS Christ, perfect man, becomes more of a man himself' (*Gaudium et spes*, §41). This belief of the Second Vatican Council is also that of all Christians who hold that the following of Christ is the way to human fulfilment for them. In the sphere of sexuality, which is the subject of this article, and keeping within the ecclesial context, the Council's words could be transposed thus: 'Whoever follows Christ as *proclaimed by his Church* becomes more of a woman or a man, attains a more joyful sexuality because it is more human.' For many decades, such an affirmation has been the subject of strong criticism both by many Christians and unbelievers. The attack made on Christian sexual morality, especially Catholic, are sufficiently well known for us not to need to spend much time on them here.[1] We need only remind ourselves that according to these critics, the ethical requirements of Christianity are the product of an obscurantism incapable of coming to terms with the discoveries of modern science; they impose unrealistic norms on people which lead to anxiety or neurosis. According to these critics ecclesial sexual morality is not very Christian because it is not very human.

Thus in our time understanding of sexuality in the light of reason alone has become the touchstone of the Christian quality of sexual life. This means that the Christian moralist, who is suspected of defending inhibiting norms, is faced with a task of apologetics. He has to show that what seems fully human to people today in sexuality is in accordance with the data of revelation or at least not contradictory to them. My object is to show that this 'demonstration' has become totally possible today, on two conditions: we must resolutely return to the biblical sources and recognise certain mistakes made by tradition in matters of sexual morality and anthropology; and we have to realise that there will still be certain divergences (both in theory and practice) between a Christian understanding of sexuality and that of a large number of our contemporaries. But precisely these divergences should alert the theologian. They may be a sign of a mistake in Christian thinking, but they may also be the symptom of a self-understanding or of behaviour of people who are alienated in ideology or in sin. This is why the moralist who is trying to show the harmony between contemporary thought on sexuality and the biblical vision cannot make the former the criterion for the truth of the latter. This would be forgetting that the Word of God is fundamentally the judge of our human 'wisdom' (1 Cor. 1). Thus the moralist has a second task: that of showing that the biblical vision, as seen through the eyes of the Church, radically challenges, on certain points, the vision of our contemporaries. This does not mean that a truly Christian sexual morality would depend on super-human norms undiscernable by reason alone, but that

51

revelation invites reason to a clearer view of the ethical blind alleys it may enter, and to free itself from obscurities which hinder it from discovering the best way in which human beings can fulfil themselves as free sexual beings.

These two tasks, of apologetics and challenge, would form a vast programme which we cannot undertake here. In this article I merely illustrate it by certain examples.

Methodological remarks

The theologian who tries to show the compatibility of the biblical vision of sexuality[2] with what appears human to our contemporaries must be aware of two facts:

1. The Bible does not offer a *single* vision of sexuality. Scripture as a whole or in any of its component books does not contain a very elaborate phenomenological or ethical reflection on sexual life. Ideas about sexuality are always expressed in the context of some theological reflection or in reply to practical questions asked by the communities or as observations on men and women's behaviour. Syntheses of biblical sexual morality thus always look a bit artificial and are in danger of being subjected to the ideological prejudices or unconscious desires of their authors. However, it is certainly possible to extract from Scripture a certain number of convictions which one cannot reject without being plainly unfaithful to the Word of God.[3] These are the convictions which the theologian should compare with contemporary anthropological convictions.

2. There is not one *single* view of sexuality. If we were tempted to forget this, the multiplicity of cultural views of sexuality would be enough to remind us. In order to make a comparison with Scripture the theologian is obliged to use what appears to him to be human in his own culture. But he quickly runs into difficulties because his own culture offers him various and sometimes even contradictory scientific and philosophical views of sexuality. To give just one example, consider the differences in both theory and therapy between the Reichian and Freudian schools, although both are popular in the West. On what basis can the theologian decree that the Freudian vision of sexuality offers a better criterion of the human than the Reichian? On the basis of a critique derived from other anthropological disciplines? But the theologian cannot be master of all these disciplines. He is therefore ill-placed to judge the validity of their critques, especially as these are disputed. Thus the theologian's choice of what is to be declared more human is likely to some extent to be a matter of chance, and determined by his point of view. His vision and judgement of some form of sexual behaviour is never an asexual one. It would therefore be false to believe that the sex of the person making the judgements is not involved in deciding what is human in sexual terms. Like all other disciplines, theology and anthropology is determined by sex. Christian morality has often made serious mistakes because it forgot this.[4]

These remarks suggest that the essentialist category of the 'human' as a criterion of Christian life in the sphere of sexuality is not immediately operative. However it is difficult to do without it. It defines the bounds of human reason in search of its full freedom. It is the starting point for the theologian's attempt to show that following Christ does correspond with the human desire for self-realisation. In fact the term 'human' which we bring to our reading of Scripture or our understanding of the Christian life is made up of a certain image of man as a sexual being, an image formed in a particular moment of history, in a particular society. The theologian also shares this image.[5] This image is based essentially on two sources: on the one hand the totality of the surest findings of divers anthropological and philosophical researches on sexuality, on the other, and perhaps more important, the sexual customs of the environment which surreptitiously impose a view of man and woman. This means that the theologian's adherence to one or another view of human sexual equilibrium is not based on evidence but on an ethical critique which results only in *moral* certainty. This, according to the expression of Olle-Laprune 'is both assent of the reason and consent of the will'. It is thus necessarily culture-bound by ideology and unconscious desires. This means that anyone who tries to criticise sexual morality must recognise that he is always duped 'to some extent', according to the usual expression of the psychoanalysts.

Thus the category 'human' in sexuality functions in a positive, critical (negative) and open way:

Positive because it indicates the necessary stages for human fulfilment, by bringing out the *invariables* to be found in every individual, whatever his or her historico-cultural conditioning[6]; if these invariables are not respected, the human being will be totally or partially destructed.

Critical or *negative* because the universal extension of the category 'human' prevents it from giving each individual, who is alway situated in time and place, a strictly defined model of sexual behaviour.[7] But also because the requirement of universality for conduct which is truly 'human' could act as a 'tribunal' to show that some particular form of sexual behaviour is incompatible with the arrival of freedom in society.[8]

The category of the 'human' is necessarily *open*, because understanding of what we are and what we might become as sexual beings must be constantly striven for, refined and modified by new knowledge, and knowledge in the sphere of sexuality is still very uncertain.

The task of the theologian is to prove that a sexual morality inspired by revelation does not invalidate, but confirms and sometimes challenges by criticism the morality constructed on the category of the 'human' seen in these terms. Let us take a few examples to show that this is possible.

Sexuality: a reminder of our finiteness

One of the strongest convictions which has arisen from the various contemporary anthropologies is this: sexuality constitutes an *essential* dimension of the human being. Biology has established that every human cell is sexually determined. Psychoanalysis shows that all human relationships in the universe, with others and with images of God are marked by sexuality. The social sciences stress that social phenomena are in close interaction with the way in which men and women assume their sexuality. Thus human beings do not exist without sexual determination. This means, among other things, that sexuality is an unsurpassable reality which constitutes one of the clearest indications of the human being's finiteness. The fact that we are sexual beings means that we are bounded by our own body with its desires. Because we are sexual beings we are radically cut off from the opposite sex,[9] while at the same time we are usually strongly attracted to it in our desire to restore a lost wholeness. Because we are sexual beings we inevitably feel sexual need, which is sometimes an extreme reminder of our dependence on others. Because we are sexual beings, we feel 'counter-order' (Lévi-Strauss) desires in ourselves, so much is sexuality bound up with violence. Because we are sexual beings, we realise that we are not *causa sui* we are the result of a meeting between two different beings . . . In short, recognising that we are sexual beings means accepting disproof of our desires for omnipotence.

We become even more aware of the link between the sexual condition and our finiteness, when we realise that sexuality is *the* 'place' of the *partial*. In fact human sexuality is not a massive biologically predetermined instinct towards a total object of the opposite sex.[10] It appears to be a more or less unstable organisation of partial drives which has arisen during the course of an often tormented development over a number of years. Clinical observation shows that even when these drives have ended up being ordered towards a partner of the opposite sex considered in his or her totality, their pressure still operates. In every human person there are partial, disordered drives.

Accepting these anthropological findings means accepting that human sexuality is a reality in the state of becoming, capable of regression, fixation, progression. We must also accept from this that there is a kinship between the normal and the abnormal and no one has his or her sexuality 'in order' once and for all.

Thus, because of the limits it imposes and because of its partial dimension affected by time, sexuality makes us recognise our finiteness. Ethical reflection which takes these anthropological data into account must state that any attempt to deny this finiteness is inhuman and cannot be tolerated.

Many of the contemporaries charge the Christian vision with precisely this denial. According to them, Christian sexual morality is founded on a mistaken view of human sexuality and on a flight from instincts, especially by the use of the theme of eschatology. They say it is incapable of getting away from the 'all or nothing' view, which leads people whose psychosexual organisation is atypical (e.g. homosexuals) to feel guilty or desperate. These criticisms are often deserved by the way some Christians speak and act. But do they really apply to a morality which was truly inspired by scripture? I do not think so.

Bible and sexuality

In the first place the Bible agrees with the contemporary view that regards sexuality as an essential dimension of the human being. We have only to re-read the two creation accounts (Gen. 1-2), to which Jesus refers in Matt. 19:4-6, to be convinced of this. These accounts have several convictions: (a) The sexual relationship between man and woman is presented both in the Yahvist and the Priestly tradition as the height of God's act of creation. It is described as very good and when Adam recognises his companion as a being who is both like and different from himself, he gives a cry of joy. (b) Sexuality is undeified and given a fully secular status. Any sacral use of sex in an attempt to reach a sort of divine omnipotence is excluded. (c) Sexuality is a mark of human contingence. This is why one of the effects of sin, which is a denial of the creaturely state, is the perversion of the relationship between man and woman (Gen. 3:7, 16).

This is as good as saying that any anthropological, theological or ethical reflection which tried to do away with sexual finiteness would be in direct contradiction with Revelation. Revelation can even contribute to helping our contemporaries guard against a devaluation of sexuality which paradoxically arises from the excessive trivialisation of its operation. In fact, scripture reminds us forcefully of the anthropological truth too often neglected today: sex is not a problem to be investigated but a mystery which involves man and woman at their deepest level. We should not over-value the use of sexuality but we must remember that it involves very important personal and collective realities. In order to live joyfully and avoid mutual violence, we must not rely on a pseudo-regulation of sexuality by itself. In fact in order to be humanising, the use of sex always requires very careful ethical regulation.

Sexuality and eschatalogy

Granted, say the critics, the Bible recognises the finiteness implied by sex. But is this recognition immediately not cancelled out by the use of the eschatological theme? For example, is consecrated celibacy not often presented by Christians as an anticipation of the eschatological life where there will be such fulness of charity that there will no longer be any need to go through the body'?[11] Does this not mean that eschatological anticipation might allow some to 'play angels', that is to fail to recognise that all human relationships, even in celibacy, bring into play partial drives whose basis is very much bodily?

We must agree that certain theological ideas of the past and the present have made use of the eschatological theme in a way that invites us to forget about sex. But this use of eschatology is not in accordance with a wise reading of Scripture. The inchoate eschatology as presented in the Bible does not require us to go beyond our bodily sexual condition and live like angels here below. It has a double operation which both confirms and makes relative our involvement in the world.

Because it is *this* world which will be transfigured in the other world, the Christian is *confirmed* in his desire to use now all his creative powers and all his sexual powers of loving. But this use takes different forms according to people's aims in life and their psycho-sexual and social conditioning. Some choose to express their acceptance of the Kingdom that comes partly by means of conjugal love. In this case they have to live fully in the three dimensions, the relational, erotic and procreative, attributed by anthropology and scripture to sexuality. Others express their discipleship of Christ in a religious or priestly life which includes celibacy, or in a life-style which forces them to make sense of unwanted celibacy. But an authentically Christian way of trying to live in continence is not to deny our bodily finiteness by anticipating a condition of the asexual risen body. It must be 'in view of the Kingdom', that is in accordance with the logic of the Kingdom of God which is a logic of service of the poor and respect for others.[13]

Eschatology also operates a *relativisation* of our way of being in the world. It reminds us 'that the form of this world is passing away' (1 Cor. 7:31) and that a Kingdom is coming in which the only law will be *agapé*. This means that sexuality is subject, no more but no less than every other human reality, to eschatological relativisation. All sexual attachments must be examined in the light of the Kingdom which is coming: emotional ties to parents, desire for or refusal of children, the way in which we take on fatherhood or motherhood, friendly or conjugal relationships. In this light it is easy to see that these ties are often over-valued or made absolute, or on the contrary, under-valued. We need only consider, for example the excessively long delay in having children on the part of many Western couples, a delay which is sometimes inhuman because it almost turns children into consumer goods.[14]

Love and law

Christian morality makes love the ultimate criterion of the quality of sexual life. This recourse to a morality of love should, apparently, finally silence those who think the Christian vision of sexuality is dehumanising. However, many anthropologists still suspect that this primacy of love is itself the cause of sexual disfunction—for various reasons which it is not possible to go into here. We merely mention, that according to certain psychoanalysts, St Augustine's aphorism 'love and do what you will' might function in a perverse manner because it could include the denial of the law. For example M. Safouan says 'what religion achieves by its absolute affirmation of love is the negation of the law.'[15] Contemporary anthropology, both in the social and the individual spheres, has shown the fundamental importance of law for the emergence of the sexual human subject. A child becomes a creature of speech, among other things, because it comes up against the taboo on incest. To become human, a man or a woman, is always by means of a process of differentiation from one's origin through the law of culture and language. The Latin etymology of the word chaste is significant in this respect: *castus* is the opposite of *incastus* (incestuous). From the point of view of a morality which takes the human fully into account, chastity is what allows a subject to live his sexuality in such a way that he constructs his relationships to others and the world in recognition of the radical differences which structure him. Thus chastity in sexuality is the refusal of omnipotence, of lack of differentiation, of imprisonment in the imaginary. We can immediately see the applications of such a vision to the different areas of life. A

E

friendship of love founded on a fusional mode is not chaste; a life which seeks to avoid all pleasure is not chaste. For pleasure, to the extent that it temporarily causes the will to lose control is a reminder of the subject's non-omnipotence. A sexual life which refuses to accept the work of time and does not tolerate the slowness of one's own or another's development or avoids all commitment, is not chaste. Parenthood which uses the child to satisfy its own desires is not chaste etc. . . . .

Does the Christian view of sexuality deny this rich anthropological notion of chastity? Certainly not! There are plenty of studies today to show that being Christian means trying to enter fully into God's creative and redeeming plan. God's creative design is presented in Scripture as a work of separation from chaos (Gen. 1) or the imposal of a prohibition (Gen. 2) which allows the recognition of the difference of the other sex and the difference of Yahweh. As for the redeeming plan, it gives back to human beings the possibility of communicating (Acts 2) among themselves and with God in a world in which sin sows confusion. The morality of love is not an invitation to the perversion of denying the rock of reality, which is difference. It is a constant invitation to take seriously all human differences including sexual differences. It is thus possible for the theologian to establish that there is a profound agreement between the ethical demands of anthropological reflection on the nature of the human sexual being and the demands of a Christianity which resolutely returns to its scriptural sources.

A morality of all or nothing?

However there still remains a radical criticism of Christian morality. Is it not all or nothing? Is it not true that millions of human beings with definitively atypical psycho-sexual organisations (homosexuality, various types of confirmed immaturity) can only find in the normalising Christian vision of morality a source of unrealistic ascesis and despair?

This is a tricky question to answer. It is undeniable that contemporary Christian talk about sex still too often assumes that all men and women, could, if they felt like it, attain a sexuality which had got over all inhibitions, compulsiveness, or fixation in an immature organisation. Christian anthropology still too often forgets that the unconscious with its many pressures exists. For example, how often moralists suggest in a unrealistic way that we should sublimate our drives. They forget that the concept of sublimation is very unprecise in Freudian theory and especially that not every one who wants to sublimate can.

The Church must seek to develop a theology and pastoral practice which takes full account of the abnormal but fixed forms that sexuality sometimes takes. However I think that any theologian who returning to the most central Christian convictions will be able to deal with this. In fact the good news that Christianity brings is that the unfortunate, the lowly, the 'lame' are the first objects of the promises of salvation. This good news also obviously applies to the 'unfortunates' in sexuality. If they listen to the word of God they can learn that holiness is within their reach through their erotic and relational disfunction. This is why a humanist Christianity does not lead to desperation but can offer a future to every man and woman. It shows that a morality in accordance with the Gospel does not require sexual 'normalisation' at any cost, but calls each person, according to his own psycho-sexual organisation, to welcome the Kingdom of God.

Translated by Dinah Livingstone

Notes

1. See e.g. J. T. Noonan *Contraception. A history of its treatment by the Catholic theologians and canonists* (Cambridge 1966); E. Fuchs *Le Désir et la tendresse* (Geneva 1979).

2. In this article, for reasons of space, I leave aside the comparison between contemporary anthropology with the data of Tradition. These have often deformed the biblical view of sexuality.

3. For example, the descralisation of sex, sexual difference as the peak of God's creative act etc.

4. Think for example, of the teachings of Tradition on women.

5. A look at Tradition shows this clearly.

6. For example: the primary drives, the prematuration of the *infans* and its consequences, the castration complex, the Oedipus complex, the necessity for the taboo on incest.

7. Which leaves room, for example, for a certain cultural pluralism in the manner in which family life is conducted.

8. For example by using the Kantian rule of universalisability, prostitution is seen to be inacceptable from the ethical point of view.

9. As the Latin etymology shows: *sexus-secare,*

10. If we accept the Freudian vision of sexuality.

11. R. Brague *La Morale, sagesse et salut* (Paris 1981).

12. With frequent reliance on a reading of Mk. 12:25 and 1 Cor. 7.

13. See further my articles 'Les célibats, risques et chances' *Etudes* (May 1980) 659-677. Here I show the ambiguity of the use of the eschatological theme for the justification of the existence of celibacy.

14. See L. Roussel and O. Bourguignon *Générations nouvelles et mariage traditionnel* (Paris 1979).

15. M. Safouan *Le Structuralisme en psychanalyse* (Paris 1968) p. 74.

Bernard Quelquejeu

Anthropological Presuppositions of Christian Existence

IS THERE such a thing as 'humanist Christianity'? In their attempts to define the meaning of this term, to eliminate all equivocal elements from it and to formulate its demands more precisely, the authors of the preceding articles have clearly demonstrated the theological importance of this theme. It is also not difficult to show that we are not concerned here in any way with an understanding of Christianity that is optional and that might be disputed and rejected even though it might not in any sense strike us as the only 'authentic' interpretation of the Christian reality. The options with which it presents us have a very restricted source—the revelation of the New Testament as understood and handed down by the apostles and embodied in early Christianity. This 'humanist Christianity' takes the spiritual reality of man very seriously because of a deep conviction that the whole of human existence is the *locus* that cannot be rejected where God must be sought and encountered. This conviction is based on two realities. The first is the incarnation of the Word of God and the second is the need for the eschatological plan of the Kingdom of God as initiated by Jesus of Nazareth to be included within the history of mankind. For all these reasons, several of the most fundamental data of the Christian tradition and of Catholic dogmatic theology as part of that tradition are involved in the 'humanist Christianity' that the other authors in this number have attempted to define.

For this reason, it would be very strange indeed if an explicit theological study of 'humanistic Christianity' had not been made until the twentieth century. In fact, the very opposite is true. Under different names and interpreted on the basis of widely divergent doctrinal presuppositions throughout the history of the Christian Church, the reality to which 'humanistic Christianity' points has continued to preoccupy the thoughts of Christians. This has happened especially, of course, when Christian theology has proved worthy of the tradition which it has inherited. As the other articles in this issue of *Concilium* have shown quite clearly, however, this does not mean that it has always been experienced in its pure form or that it has at every period in the history of Christianity been the only Christian understanding of this phenomenon.

In this article, I shall try to show, with the help of two examples which I have chosen from a great number which might have been equally illuminating, how this understanding, which corresponds to what we would call nowadays 'humanist Christianity', has been expressed at different periods in the history of the Church and

58

therefore in different cultural and philosophical contexts. The first example that I have chosen is Thomas Aquinas' teaching as expressed in the theological axiom *gratia praesupponit naturam*. The second is the modern example of Karl Rahner's 'transcendental theology'. These two examples are, in my opinion, particularly useful not only because of their intrinsic theological value, but also because they are closely interrelated. It is not my intention, in discussing the first example in some detail and the second a little more cursorily, to look at them in the light of the history of Christian doctrines. My principal intention is to conform to the requirements of the third part of this number of *Concilium* and therefore to throw light on this whole theological theme and to review critically its conditions and its limitations.

1. THOMAS AQUINAS' AXIOM *GRATIA PRAESUPPONIT NATURAM*

Everyone who has read Thomas' *Summa* will recall the little sentence *gratia praesupponit naturam*, sometimes given as *gratia non tollit, non destruit, sed perficit naturam*. It is remarkable that Thomas never provides an explanation of this principle, but uses it as something that is already well known when he wants to establish a connection between some aspects of the so-called 'natural' realities and the corresponding aspect of the realities of grace. One has the impression that this is one of the common-places which is repeated by all theologians and which expresses no more than a vague concept of unity between the work of God as the creator and author of 'natural' realities and the work of the same God as revealed in Jesus Christ in his proposition of grace.[1]

It is, in fact, a structural principle of that work, the justification of which is the outcome of the whole of the doctrine which can be formed from the explicit use of the axiom. There are explicit references to the axiom in six main spheres. These are the relationships between a natural knowledge of God and the knowledge of faith, between natural love and charity, between the created essence of the soul and grace, between the natural law and divine law, between free will and the freedom of grace and finally the sphere of the harm to 'human nature' caused by sin. The whole doctrine is synthesised in Thomas' teaching about the image of God.

Using this axiom, Thomas tries to provide a theological justification for the difference and the unity between human nature on the one hand and grace on the other. The axiom can therefore be interpreted in these two ways, which are not, however, equal to one another. The more basic and original interpretation, which is in accordance with the use of the verb *praesupponit*, is the theological understanding of certain demands made by the natural order on the basis of realities of grace, following the approach from grace to nature. This affirms that the gifts of salvation are firmly anchored in adequate natural structures which are also given their ultimate meaning and value there.

The movement from nature to grace, on the other hand, which is in accordance with the use of the verb *perficit*, is only secondary and is ultimately based on the primary structure that is established in the original meaning. This movement is often combined with the use of the analogy of faith, which in this case forms one of its foundations. The natural analogy, which is employed in an attempt to explain one aspect of the revealed mystery, expresses within the natural order the structure that is obeyed in the order of grace by the supernatural reality. This takes place above all in anthropology. The supernatural call to lead the same life as God and to 'participate' in the nature of God himself is in no sense alien to the mysterious intuitions of our own humanity and is in a way a response to the aspirations that form part of the dynamism of human subjectivity. The way in which man accomplishes his supernatural vocation is in no sense contradictory to, but is in fact united very closely with the way in which man fulfils himself through his natural conditions. This is why the movement from nature to grace, which frequently covers the same ground as the movement of the natural analogy, is ultimately based on the presupposition that is expressed by the interpretation of the axiom in the direction of grace to nature. The opposite and reciprocal movement backwards and forwards, from grace to nature and from nature to grace, enables us to speak theologically, that is, about the one God of creation and the covenant of grace.

Let us now consider the anthropological claims regarding man as a created spirit, which Thomas viewed differently according to the sphere which he had in mind. Together, these claims constitute a configuration of the relationships between a theological anthropology and a philosophy of man or the human spirit.

The application of the axiom to the sphere of knowledge[2] points in the first place to an ordered duality in the object of faith—the characteristic object of the knowledge of faith presupposes, if it is to be intrinsically constituted and therefore reached by human understanding, the presence in it of an underlying object of natural knowledge. In the second place, the axiom affirms that, far from destroying the natural functioning of knowledge because it requires it to be used, the knowledge of faith fulfils its potentialities in quite a new way. Within this second meaning, the axiom also affirms, on the basis of faith, the demands made and the structure presupposed by a faculty of the human mind that is, in accordance with its own resources, capable of a certain intellectual insight into God that is open to the supernaturalisation of faith.

The application of the axiom to man's spiritual appetite[3] gives emphasis to the fact that the theology virtue of charity is given a welcoming structure by the natural dynamism of that spiritual appetite and this structure acts as a guarantee that man will make real use of it. This dynamism is partly impaired by original sin. It is also defined as a movement that forms part of the texture of the spiritual appetite, not only as a necessary and implicit propensity, but also as a natural disposition to love freely, deliberately and explicitly that is linked with a similarly natural disposition to know. For all these reasons, this natural dynamism has its own potentialities and original dispositions and these are included within the theological virtue of charity which 'fulfils' this natural ability to seize God effectively.

These two applications to the axiom—to the sphere of knowledge and to man's spiritual appetite—originate and are united in the application at the most fundamental level, that of the realtionship between created grace and its subject.[4] Created grace, in the form in which the theologian is obliged to conceive it if he is to understand what is provided by revelation, finds in man's most fundamental constitution, the essence of his soul as the principle in which all his active powers are rooted, a welcoming structure which acts as a guarantee for man's adequate ontological appropriation. This is where the demands made and the structure presupposed by man's spritiual nature have their basis.

Thomas also speaks of other applications of this axiom which are intrinsically important. These include, for example, the part played by the natural law as a presupposition of the divine law[5] and the function of free will as the basis of the freedom of grace.[6] These are, however, only consequences of the preceding theological affirmations. The latter are firmly united and therefore synthesised in the way in which man as spirit is called the 'image of God'. This image exists at various levels.[7] The 'first image' is man's constitution with a natural disposition to know and love God and therefore to be in communion with him. This 'first image' is the presupposition for the 'second image', which points to the realisation of this destiny to be in communion with God through faith and charity in an incipient way and through the beatific vision and union as the fulfilment. (This is the 'third image'.) Because of his spiritual nature, man is therefore affirmed as formally ready to receive the grace of salvation.

The theological principles that are involved in this axiom 'grace presupposes nature' therefore govern some of the most profound options in Thomas' thought. The axiom conceals a doctrinal and methodological dimension which in fact goes beyond what is suggested by the explicit quotations. It is possible to confirm this on the basis of several implicit applications of these principles.

The questions raised by the limits of man's natural powers to act, in his concrete state here and now with his nature marked with the stain of original sin, mean that the damage caused by the sin of our original parents to the ontological constitution of man's nature, which is therefore 'fallen', has to be examined. In his own characteristic form of expression, Pseudo-Dionysius provided the authority that was required, but, despite this, the implications of the axiom itself form the most important elements in Thomas' teaching about this question. Sin cannot destroy the constitutive principles of this ontological structure without at the same time destroying the created subject himself and therefore changing his species. It can, however, impair him by diminishing his dynamic capacity and correlatively the unity of his powers to act. The negative drama of sin requires in human nature the same presuppostions as the positive adventure of grace and holiness, but it carves out in reverse the very features that are outlined in relief by grace and holiness.[8]

It is always this axiom which determines both the expression, in terms of supernatural *habitus*, and the divine gift of the theological and the infused virtues and the correct view of the relationships between supernatural infused virtue and the natural acquired virtue. Our understanding of the hylemorphic constitution of the sacraments is also connected with this. The way in which man carries out his supernatural vocation does not reject, but on the contrary fully accepts the way in which he is, because of his natural state, the active principle of his own action, with the result that the initial passivity, in accordance with which man welcomes the new gift of God, becomes a dynamic activity and a collaboration in the process of 'deification'. Even the paths by which grace normally comes to man—in other words, the channels of sacramentality—respect human nature by assuming man's fleshly nature and by urging him to respond to the divine movement of grace by a human approach which will take hold of him in every part of his being—body and soul, sense and spirit and intelligence and appetite. Grace, then, not only presupposes, but also respects and fulfils nature.

The reader who has compared Thomas' doctrine to which the axiom 'grace presupposes nature' refers with the perspectives that have been disclosed by 'humanist Christianity' will undoubtedly have been struck by a certain connection between the two, despite their differences. At the same time, it is important not to minimise these differences. The whole of Thomas' apparatus seems to us today to be alien—his enormous confidence in metaphysics with an ontological tendency, his repeated use of the concept of 'nature', even in its opposition to the concept of grace and his inclination to treat man, his cognitive faculties and his appetites formally and not to take into account the many concrete spheres in which those faculties and appetites are expressed, that is, the spheres of work, sexuality, politics, leisure and culture. Nonetheless, it is difficult to deny that, although he uses quite different concepts from those employed today, Thomas still to great extent includes what is contained in the contemporary theories of 'humanist Christianity' within his teaching based on the axiom 'grace presupposes nature'. He takes the human phenomenon very seriously. He affirms that, on the basis of human free will and man's own dynamic forces, it is man himself who is the 'subject' of the adventure of grace. He is convinced that, however original it may be, man's knowledge of God cannot break the rules governing all knowledge. He is certain that the theological virtue of charity cannot disregard man's most radical affective dynamism. He is also convinced that man's divine and Christian vocation takes place in the way in which he expresses himself as a man through the state into which he was born. Although its cultural and anthropological framework is quite different, does 'humanist

Christianity' really say anything radically different from this? Is, in my case, what I have said so far about Thomas' teaching not enough to justify the claims that a thorough knowledge of that teaching and especially of his theological anthropology might make an important contribution to a reasonable and balanced elaboration of 'humanist Christianity'?

2. MAN AS OPEN TO THE DIVINE MYSTERY ACCORDING TO KARL RAHNER

My second example, which I shall discuss more briefly on the assumption that the reader is more familiar with it, is Karl Rahner's 'transcendental theology', with its very obvious links with the Thomist theology outlined above.

Rahner's teaching can be more readily understood if it is considered in connection with the works of M. Blondel and J. Maréchal. Blondel was opposed to the extrinsic character of classical Catholic apologetics, according to which Christian faith was based on external signs such as miracles and prophecies. He therefore tried to show, by philosophical argument in L'Action (1893) and the Lettre (1896), that it is a datum of the human spirit that it is orientated towards the supernatural because of an inner and necessary 'demand' and that it is therefore possible to establish a connection of intimate communication between man's spiritual nature and divine grace. In its formal necessity, the supernatural can only be understood as a response to the fulfilment of the human spirit. This sovereign relationship, which Blondel established by his 'method of immanence', is the necessary presupposition for a historical religion if it is to provide man with the concrete response that is 'demanded' by his spiritual nature. In an attempt to safeguard the 'gratuitous' nature of salvation, Blondel was careful to show that the necessary orientation of the spirit towards this response of revelation as found in history did not in any way imply that the response should be regarded as subordinate to man's needs and therefore as conditioned by anthropological categories.

In his Le point de départ de la métaphysique (1926), Maréchal attempted to reconcile the 'realistic' metaphysical approach of Thomism with the 'reflective' transcendental method of the philosophy of the spirit of the German and in particular Kantian idealists. He succeeded in showing that the metaphysical and the transcendental methods were, in the case of every object of immanent activity, necessarily both legitimate and complementary and that each method postulated the other.

Not only in his great works Geist in Welt and Hörer des Wortes, but also in many other publications, Karl Rahner has tried to extend the train of thought initiated by Maréchal. In this, he has been especially influenced by Heidegger's existential philosophy. In his search for the religious meaning of the 'nostalgia' that characterises human existence, Rahner has analysed the paradox of the human condition. Man controls everything because of his ability to make abstractions and to judge, to accept or reject and to love or hate and because of this he is conscious of being a 'subject'. At the same time, however, he is made to be a body and is therefore immersed in what is visible and tangible and is, in other words, a spirit in the world. A recognition of the finite nature of every object of thought, love or the will is at least an implicit affirmation that the infinite is implied in all our human processes. The one who is infinitely 'different'—God—is therefore recognised as the a priori condition of our finite spirit. He is the horizon in which everything is included as the condition of 'transcendental' possibility of all our acts of knowledge and freedom. That is why, as a spiritual being, man has, in every concrete experience, something at least akin to a 'transcendental' experience of God. This certainly does not mean that, even if he is always already 'present', in a presence that is not objectivised, in the fulfilment of the spirit by itself, God is at the same time the object of explicit knowledge. Knowledge of God calls for an analysis and a reflection. The integral development of this analysis is found in transcendental theology, which has shown that there is, in the depths of the human subject's experience of his own fulfilment, an initial 'revelation' of God. This is a 'universal revelation'. Because God wants to save all men, man experiences himself in the concrete under the impulse of supernatural grace. God created man with the intention of giving himself to him. As a consequence, if all God's decrees necessarily have an effect, man should be *able* to receive this love which is God himself. He must be able to accept it as one who has room and scope, understanding and desire for it.[9] This real and lasting capacity is something that is most intimately and personally man's—the centre and the foundation of what he is absolutely (*ibid*, p. 311). This factual destiny cannot be 'natural', that is, it cannot constitute human nature as such, although it is an internal constitutive element of his concrete essence (*ibid*, p. 302). Rahner here returns to the theological practice of generalised transcendental analysis and speaks of man's 'supernatural existential aspect'.

In speaking of this 'universal revelation'—or transcendental revelation—Rahner situates the necessity of historical revelation in man's essentially historical condition. Man is 'open' to the Word of God, but this comes to him in human words and can only be heard in the fabric of history and within a revelation that takes place in history. This does not in any sense mean that our historical realisation and our definitive social representation of God should be simply a concrete expression of the 'universal' or 'transcendental' revelation of God. From the moment that God's communication of himself was established as a historical manifestation, that self communication has first and foremost affirmed the reality of God. This is what Rahner has always striven to express in his presentation of the historical transcendental element as the 'real symbol' of the transcendental element. Without this 'concrete affirmation' in history, the transcendental element would not be 'real'. Rahner often uses this fundamental concept of an 'ontology of the symbol' as the principle by which many theological problems can be solved.

Rahner goes on to say that the historico-categorial manifestation of God's transcendental revelation reached its zenith in Jesus Christ. In the revelation of Jesus Christ God communicated himself in a 'definitive and insurpassable' manner, because he took the stature and the history of the man Jesus as his own stature and his own history. Man, who is, according to Rahner, open to the 'divine mystery', is made finally transcendent in the person of the Saviour. The insurpassable unity between nature and grace, man's aspiration and God's gift, history and revelation is fulfilled in the 'distinct and inseparable unity between God and man in Jesus Christ', that is, in this historically definitive 'real symbol' of God.

It is not difficult to see that Rahner's transcendental theology, of which I have given a very bare outline here, culminates in an interpretation of human 'existence', which is precisely what Thomas Aquinas was aiming to achieve in his theology based on the axiom 'grace presupposes nature'. The experience of transcendence implied in the fulfilment of human freedom, which is the foundation of all activity on the part of man's spirit and the condition that makes that activity possible, is therefore the horizon of our everyday human existence in history. That is why it is the 'first and particular *locus* of the reality of Christianity'. What, we may ask in this context, does 'Christianity' mean? Rahner's reply to this question is: 'Considered as a *reality*, it is simply our precise experience of this transcendence, . . . but, considered as *teaching*, it is simply our correct interpretation of that transcendental experience and its development as a whole'.[10] It is clear, then, that there is an essential affinity between Rahner's transcendental theology and what we have, in this issue of *Concilium*, called 'humanist Christianity'.

3. SOME CONCLUSIONS

It is rather surprising that Rahner's very powerful idea has hardly been echoed at all in recent Catholic dogmatic theology, especially since those specialising in that theology frequently turn to Rahner for a solution to many theological problems. The reason may perhaps be that Rahner's transcendental theology is both formal and abstract. His placing of the ultimate unity of reality in human subjectivity has also been criticised. Theologians are at the present time confronted with the history of the human spirit, the criticism of society and the social philosophies of history, as represented, for example, in the writings of Bloch, Adorno, Horkheimer and Benjamin. Many of them tend to reiterate in their own way the Hegelian attempt to go beyond Kant's philosophy and therefore have abandoned the transcendental subject, because they are critical of the way in which that subject is alienated from the world and history. Many others have at the same time also abandoned another tendency in theology which is also associated with important figures and is based on intersubjectivity, claiming that it does not avoid the danger of 'privatising' the believing subject and of separating him from society. The true subject of Christian faith should not, they insist, be considered apart from his practical and existential relationship with the political and social reality.

That is why, as soon as they have become familiar with the important lessons that can be learnt from the Thomist theology and its extension in Rahner's theology, those who insist on a 'humanist Christianity' will look for new ways forward. The particular *locus* of Christianity is not simply the spiritual fulfilment of the individual subject (even though it is this in a very radical way), nor is it the expressions of interpersonal love, even when this is extended to include the greater dimensions of intersubjectivity. It is rather in the universal reconciliation of the social reality in history and in the history of suffering. Only this reconciliation, which is the object of an apocalyptic hope that includes the fulfilment of the state of being as a subject of everyone, including the forgotten people, those who are crushed and those who have died, constitutes an adequate, collective and universal subject for Christian faith. In Jesus Christ and in the history of his disciples, this subject is already on the way to fulfilment. This is the field in which those who want to experience the reality and reflect about the theology of 'humanist Christianity' should be working today.

Translated by David Smith

Notes

1 I have made use here of the results of a thesis presented at the Saulchoir for the degree of reader in theology in 1964; it exists in typescript in the library of the Saulchoir: '*Gratia praesupponit naturam*'. *L'anthropologie comme projet théologique*.

2. *In III Sent.* d. 24, q. 1, a. 3, sol. 1, ad 3; *In Boeth. de Trin.* q. 2, a. 3, responsio; *De Ver.* q. 14, a. 9, ad 8; q. 14, a. 10, ad 4; q. 14, a. 10, ad 9; *ST* Ia. q. 1, a. 8, ad 2; q. 2, a. 2, ad 1; q. 62, a. 7, ad 2; q. 62, a. 7, ad 2; q. 62, a. 7 sed c.; *ST* IIa, IIae. q. 10, a. 1, ad 1; *ST* IIIa. q. 71, ad 1; etc.

3. *ST* Ia, q. 1, a. 8, ad 2; q. 60, a. 5, c.; q. 62, a. 7 sed c.; *ST* IIa, IIae, p. 26, a. 3, c.; q. 26, a. 9, obj. 2; *De Car.* q. un., a. 8, ad 7; etc.

4. *In II Sent.* d. 26, q. un., a. 3, obj. 1; a. 4, obj. 2; *In IV Sent.* d. 4, q. 1, a. 3, qula 1, c. and ad 2; *De Ver.* q. 27, a. 6, ad 1 and ad 3; *De Malo* q. 2, a. 11, c.; etc.

5. *ST* Ia IIae. q. 99, a. 2, ad 1; *ST* IIa, IIae, q. 10, a. 10; c.; q. 22, a. 1, c.; etc.

6. *De Ver.* q. 24, a. 8, obj. 1 and ad 6; *De Malo* q. 7, a. 7, obj. 10 and ad 10; etc.

7. See, for example *ST* Ia, q. 93, a. 4. See also Thomas' use of the phrase *capax Dei* in *De Ver.* q. 27, a. 7, obj. 2; *ST* IIIa. q. 23, a. 3, ad 3; q. 6, a. 2, c.; *ST* Ia, IIae. q. 113, a. 10, c.; q. 110, a. 4, obj. 3; etc.

8. '"Naturalia manent integra": contribution à l'étude de la portée méthodologique et doctrinale d'un axiome théologique' *RSPT* 49 (1965) 640-655.

9. 'Concerning the Relationship between Nature and Grace' *Theological Investigations* (London 1961) I p. 311.

10. *Est-il possible aujourd'hui de croire?* (Paris 1966) p. 122-123.

Christian Duquoc

The Folly of The Cross
and 'The Human'

IN ABOUT 180 A.D., the philosopher Celsus wrote of Christians: 'Their injunctions are like this. "Let no one educated, no one wise, no one sensible draw near. For these abilities are thought by us to be evils. But as for anyone ignorant, anyone stupid, anyone uneducated, anyone who is a child, let him come boldly." By the fact that they themselves admit that these people are worthy of God, they show that they want and are able to convince only the foolish, dishonourable and stupid, and only slaves, women, and little children.'[1]

Their ideology, he points out, is illustrated by the social composition of Christian groups: 'In private houses also we see wool-workers, cobblers, laundry-workers, and the most illiterate and bucolic yokels . . .'[2]

An even stranger paradox, he notes, is that 'Those who summon people to the other mysteries make this preliminary proclamation: Whosoever has pure hands and a wise tongue. And again, others say: Whosoever is pure from all defilement, and whose soul knows nothing of evil, and who has lived well and righteously.'[3] But the Christians do very differently: 'Whosoever is a sinner, they say, whosoever is unwise, whosoever is a child, and, in a word, whosoever is a wretch, the kingdom of God will receive him.'[4]

Celsus is here taking obvious delight in echoing the words of Paul in 1 Cor. 1:17-26: 'For Christ did not send me to baptise but to preach the gospel, and not with eloquent wisdom, lest the cross of Christ be emptied of its power. For the word of the cross is folly to those who are perishing, but to us who are being saved it is the power of God. For it is written, "I will destroy the wisdom of the wise, and the cleverness of the clever I will thwart." Where is the wise man? Where is the scribe? Where is the debater of this age? Has not God made foolish the wisdom of the world? For since, in the wisdom of God, the world did not know God through wisdom, it pleased God through the folly of what we preach to save those who believe. For Jews demand signs and Greeks seek wisdom, but we preach Christ crucified, a stumbling block to Jews and folly to Gentiles, but to those who are called, both Jews and Greeks, Christ the power of God and the wisdom of God. For the foolishness of God is wiser than men, and the weakness of God is stronger than men.'

The repercussions this text was to have in Christian tradition are well enough known.

65

To illustrate them I will quote Luther's thesis 20 from the Heidelberg Disputation of 26 April 1518: 'But he is rightly called a theologian who understands that part of God's being which is visible and directed towards the world to be presented in suffering and in the cross. That part of God's being which is visible and directed towards the world is opposed to what is invisible, his humanity, his weakness, his foolishness . . . For as men misused the knowledge of God on the basis of his works, God again willed that he should be known from suffering, and therefore willed to reject such wisdom of the invisible by a wisdom of the visible, so that those who did not worship God as he is manifested in his works might worship him as the one who is hidden in suffering (I Cor. 1:21). So it is not enough and no use for anyone to know God in his glory and his majesty if at the same time he does not know him in the lowliness and shame of his cross . . . Thus true theology and true knowledge of God lie in Christ the crucified one.'[5]

This issue of *Concilium* has as its title: *'The Human', Criterion of Christian Existence?* The question mark included shows that this title is meant as a hypothesis. But the choice of the adjectival noun 'the human' is pre-emptive: 'the human' cannot be replaced in the title by its contemporary, 'the inhuman', or its transcendent derivative, 'the superhuman'. For Celsus, Christianity was inhuman because the message it proclaimed and the behaviour that was grounded in it were unworthy of God; this inhumanity, which was demonstrated by the social status of its adherents, followed logically in his view from the inhumanity of its Witness, the Crucified one. By shattering the harmony between the human and the divine as the sages lived and defined it, Christianity had slandered God. For Paul on the contrary, and, later on, for Luther, this slander was the touchstone of true knowledge of God, because it was bound up with the cross of Christ. Who is human? The sage for whom the cross is unworthy of God? Paul or Luther for whom the cross is the necessary passageway to any true knowledge of God and is therefore also, as they unquestioningly assume, the necessary passageway to any true humanity?

The noun 'cross' is just as ambiguous and unclear as the adjective 'human'. Linguistically, the cross is used on two levels, figuratively, in the metaphor, and concretely, to refer to Jesus' death on the cross. The expression 'carrying one's cross' is metaphorical, even though it is based on the historical occurrence. As a metaphor, the cross expresses renunciation of the world and the positive integration into the search for God of suffering and all that is negative. Now, renunciation is not in itself inhuman: 'I' can only emerge from 'that' if my impulses are brought under control by a process akin to the travail of bereavement. Any therapy that leads to a balanced personality, like any policy that aims at social peace, includes renunciation, since it is a necessary stage in the attainment of humanity, for individuals and societies alike. The metaphor of the cross transforms what is negative into a positive road to God; but is it used only in this developmental, 'therapeutic' sense? I shall examine this question in the first main part of my article.

The cross is also a historical event. It is as such an event that it figures in the Confession of Faith, since the Church proclaims that Jesus' death on the cross took place 'once and for all' by situating it in time: 'he died under Pontius Pilate'. Is the interpretation the metaphor gives of this event a legitimate one? The second main section of my article will be devoted to this question.

1. THE CROSS AS A METAPHOR

I do not intend to join in the semantic and semiotic arguments about metaphor. To readers who wish to pursue the question I recommend P. Ricoeur's *Le Métaphor vive*[6] and, to save time, will take as my starting-point the definition of metaphor in the Thesarus of the *Encyclopedia Universalis*[7] which reads: 'metaphor consists in presenting one idea via the sign of another idea which has no connection with the first beyond some conformity or analogy . . . Both by the extent of its field of application and by the absence of rules governing its construction, metaphor can immediately be seen to be a mode of expression which leaves complete freedom of scope to imagination and invention. The process of metaphorisation thus consists in connecting two terms by some analogy and submitting one of the terms for the other . . . It then becomes clear that a symptom is a metaphor, if one moves from the linguistic process to the study of its roots in the unconscious.'

I am applying this rhetorical process to the cross for the very simple reason that the cross has become the symbol which indentifies Christians. Their recognition signal is the sign of the cross. In common parlance this sign is synonymous with suffering, trouble, sickness and death—but non-pejoratively. It revalues life's hard blows and even its injustices; it gives value to what is negative, allows the failures or misfortunes that beset any human life to be positively assumed. Thus the cross, a specific, concrete instrument of torture, a sign of degradation and of shame, has become the sign of the true path to God in so far as that path requires that the negative be accepted, if not actually occasioned. When it is challenged through the cross, the negative is transmuted into a positive value. The cross thus functions as a metaphor in which the vast realm of the negative emerges as the area where redemption takes place.

As a metaphor, the cross serves as a short-circuiting device to present as positive aspects of life that are otherwise thought of or experienced as undesirable, harmful and negative. By this subtle trick of metaphor, the cross successfully transfers onto the human plane things we instinctively find inhuman; and having by its power of transmutation brought about this transference, it then gives them special status as the primary road to God.

This whole operation can be performed only if there is a process of selection, that is to say if some one element is made pre-eminent or dominant. The metaphor does this by separating the cross from the crucifixion, that historically identifiable act which, by way of a judicial trial, was the consequence of Jesus' attitudes, activities and words. The metaphor forgets about the crucifixion and gives pre-eminence to the cross, which it sets up as the symbol of misfortune and suffering and makes into a value in its own right, obliterating everything that actually led up to it and transformed its original social significance. Occasionally, the metaphor may be brought to life by recollection of Jesus' death on the cross, but as soon as the crucifixion is forgotten and the metaphor becomes dominant, the social implications of the cross are changed.

As a metaphor, the cross thus has a dual role. On the one hand, it is the metaphor of renunciation, of the ascesis necessary for drawing near God; it conveys in concrete terms that there can be no meeting with God without a painful parting from self. It breaks with the here-and-now of the satisfaction afforded by the senses, the imagination, the intellect. It gives positive value to what is instinctively seen as destructive. In this use of the metaphor, the cross represents a dynamic process, the difficult process of self-construction in relation to the Other.

On the other hand, the cross is the metaphor of resignation and at times of 'dolarism', i.e. of belief in the usefulness and necessity of suffering. The sign of salvation becomes acceptance of suffering, not rebellion against suffering; resignation to poverty and submission in the face of exploitation by the powerful. This apparent justification of poverty and submission was at times forcefully criticised in the past and is being so criticised today. The following quotation from the marxist writer Henri Lefebvre's *Critique de la vie quotidienne*[8] describes how religion is used to justify social submissiveness; the cross serves as a metaphor representing acceptance of the inhuman, and encourages alienation and exploitation.

After describing the cross-shaped village church, Lefebvre adds:

'Now I see the terrifying depths . . . of man's alienation. For century after century, oh Holy Church, you have been sucking in and storing up all men's illusions, all their fictions, all their empty hopes, all their powerlessness. You gather them in to your houses like a priceless harvest, and every generation of men, every age, every stage of human life brings something to your storerooms. Here I can see the terrors of childhood; here, the anxieties of adolescence; here, the hopes and doubts that come with the prime of life, and even the frights and the despair of old age, for you can afford, at no cost to yourself, to say that the evening of the world is drawing near and that the now aging human race will perish unfulfilled. A few men step aside from life in order to gain the power to dominate life with an art that feeds on the experience of twenty centuries and more. And because they are consecrated to the absolute these men seem sacred . . . And they watch with concern over the new-born babe's first breath and the last gasp of the dying, over children's questions and virgins' fears, over the turmoil of adolescents, over the worries of the poor and even the sorrows of the mighty; wherever there is human weakness, they are there. Everything—including doubt and heresy, and direct attack—is put to use by this old, ever wilier experience, this "spiritual" body of the Church. It is just a limitless capacity for absorbing and accumulating the inhuman: nothing less and nothing more. Oh, I know what they claim, because they have "broadened" their positons on this point too, in an attempt to absorb the enemy. The Church has condemned modernism ten times over, and now it is trying to be "modern". The most subtle of its servants will say (are already saying) that it encapsulates man's progress towards the Divine, man's age-old effort to reach beyond himself, and the slow revelation of the divine. No! No, you are but alienation, rendering from self, compelling allurement. I see it writ plain on the walls of this village church. I can read there a précis of your history, which is the history of human wretchedness! I can see summed up on those walls all your experience, all your art of domination, of preserving whole and entire the inhuman monolith that presses down on mankind like some monstrous, growing, living, thing. You served the Roman emperors, the feudal lords, the absolute monarchs and the triumphant bourgeois. And every time (with some clever discreet manoeuvring to show your own independence and your own superiority) you were on the side of the mighty, and were mightier than them because you made it appear that you were defending the weak. And now you would have us believe you are taking up the cause of Man, that is to say the cause of yesterday's oppressed who have become the mighty of tomorrow? No. This stratagem is far too obvious . . .'

Here the Christ is symbolised by the cross on which the ground-plan of its places of worship is based. Does this use of the metaphor of human wretchedness to support domination have any connection with the underlying event, the death of Jesus of Nazareth? The metaphor provides scope for the imagination and invention, but does it not by-pass the message inherent in the crucifixion? Does the metaphor of the cross really transcribe what the apostle Paul calls the folly of the cross? If the relation between the cross as it lives on in metaphor and the history of Jesus of Nazareth from which it grew is to be judged dispassionately, it is essential that we study the meaning of Jesus' crucifixion and death.

2. THE CROSS AS A HISTORICAL EVENT

At the heart of the metaphor of the cross dwells a historical event: the crucifixion of Jesus. This event allegedly validates marking the negative as positive because the Son of God, a perfect model, renounced his right to live by freely choosing the way of the cross. In *Crucifixion*,[9] M. Hengel gives a realistic account of what death by the cross involved in antiquity. He sets the crucifixion against its cultural, social and political background and so makes one realise how shameful, horrible and cruel it was. Yet stressing the descriptive details may be a subtle means of rejecting its historic import and giving substance to a pre-established theory. In this theory, the historical occurrence is used as a metaphor for a drama that takes place between God and God, with the Son giving his life to pay the debt that man owes God, and that God in his terrible justice cannot remit. The description of the horrors of the cross is aimed solely at revealing the implacability of divine justice, which, if we are to be absolved, demands nothing less than the life of an innocent man in place of ours. When the death on the cross is interpreted like this, it backs up the metaphor, since its authority validates the use of the cruel death of the Son of God to show that all must follow the negative and painful way of the cross. But is it the event that dictates this interpretation? Could it not be the metaphor that is leaving its impress on the event?

The historical event of the cross is part of the Confession of Faith, in which we proclaim that Jesus died for us. It is because it is so confessed that the crucifixion ceases to be an insignificant incident; were it not for the Confession of Faith the crucifixion of Jesus would have been forgotten, like that of the thousands who died on a cross in antiquity and whom no one now remembers. The death of Jesus, which in its day was no more than a commonplace murder, is transformed by remembrance in the Confession into a focal point for mankind, the point on which interpretation of the future of man in relation to God must centre. The cross of Jesus is a fundamental part of the Christian revelation of God. Emphasising its descriptive details leads to an interpretation heavy with consequence; it is therefore essential to show how the immanent logic of the historical process which led to the cross led also to its being recognised as having universal import.

In the Confession of Faith, the event of the cross is interpreted soberly: Jesus died under Pontius Pilate, for us, for our sins and for our salvation. The Confession presents the death of Jesus as having universal application, as concerning the destiny of every human being. By confessing the Cross, it makes the Cross a linguistic event, and so breaks it wide open, rescuing it from being a self-insulated, individual event or just another anecdote. Because of the Confession, the death on the cross cannot be reduced to the status of a minor incident, an accident or an unfortunate misunderstanding. As I have said, thousands underwent this torment, but their names have not come down through history. Their deaths, being remembered in no Confession of Faith, remain imprisoned in their individuality.

The Confession of Faith is not an abstract proclamation, but depends on the fourfold narrative of the Gospels. The fact that through the Confession the cross changes status and takes on universal significance in itself explains nothing: it invites us to reread the narratives which recount the event within the overall framework of Jesus' life and preaching. These narratives tell of the suffering and death of someone whose actions and passions we proclaim in the Confession to be of universal import. But the Confession is valueless without the narrative, and the narrative lives through the Confession. Because of the differing approaches, the narrative can be variously interpreted, and imposes in faith only what is proclaimed in the Confession; but that it imposes as the developing pattern of Jesus' life, culminating in a trial and the cross. By making Jesus' death part of the enactment of his life, the narrative rules out a gnostic interpretation. The question that should be examined if one is attempting to clarify the relation between the metaphor of the cross and the historical event of the cross seems to me to be this: do the Gospel narratives of the passion and death of Jesus really contain at their heart the issues that dominate the metaphor? That is, is the 'inhuman' I have found myself obliged to see in the metaphor justified by the narratives? Or do the narratives point towards a different interpretation of the cross and suggest that it has a different social function?

In the space of an article I can give little more than the outline of an answer to this question. It will be developed in three stages: (*a*) the passion narratives do not validate the metaphor; (*b*) the passion narratives cannot be separated from the overall development of the gospels; (*c*) the passion narratives show that Jesus died because he broke with the logic immanent in oppressive violence. When these three stages of the answer have been clarified, it will be possible to demonstrate that the Cross and 'the human' are not contradictory, but belong together.

(*a*) The passion narratives do not validate the metaphor

The metaphor cunningly expresses a social or psychological position the real issue of which is obscured. At the heart of the metaphor of the cross lies an event, the cross of a certain Jesus, around which the metaphor is tacitly constructed. But the presence of Jesus' cross at the heart of the metaphor is occluded by the fact that the metaphor indiscriminately presents as a positive way of approach to God any aspect of human life that is felt as negative. Once the metaphor takes over from the historical event, we have to ask: who is using it? Who is it that is praising the cross? When it is the person carrying it, the praise is much more credible than when it comes from someone who is standing at a distance. The historical event makes us think of him who carried it, Jesus of Nazareth, but once we lose sight of him, the cross becomes an abstraction, because the metaphor inverts its social and effective function. The passion narratives are not a metaphorical illustration of non-specific suffering; they are an account of the path Jesus of Nazareth was led to by the prophetic and messianic choice he had adopted.

(*b*) The passion narratives are inseparable from the overall development of the gospels

Some metaphorically based theological interpretations of the cross give it such prominence that Jesus' life up to that point is left quite out of account. This approach is wrong, because the cross is the outcome of a trial, the outcome, that is, of an accusation based on acts he had committed or actions wrongly attributed to him. Jesus was brought gradually to the point of standing trial by his opposition to elements of Jewish tradition that were considered fundamental in his time; those responsible for handing this tradition on correctly found his words and actions unacceptable. I will mention only one point on which he opposed the accepted view: he went counter to the established practice by proclaiming boldly to all outcasts, that is, to sinners or people whose way of life or place in society caused them to be seen as sinners, that for the God he was preaching their rejection was meaningless. To the pious who strove sincerely to adhere to a pure and strict religion in their daily lives and not to be like the rest of men—the multitude who thought the demands of religion were excessive—this so radically different view of the consequences of religious practice was an outrage. In the eyes of the religious authorities Jesus came more and more to be a misfit, while the multitude, faced with the messianic options he presented, began to waver. In the end, he who had fought the casting out of others found himself an outcast: his death on the cross was the consequence of his being rejected by the community into which he was born.

The cross was the result of this whole process of development; if the two are dissociated, it loses all christic meaning, for Jesus died because he fought for justice.

(*c*) Jesus died because he broke with oppressive violence

Some theological theories leave aside the prophetic development which led to his being tried and condemned, and fail to bring out the fundamental role it played in his death; rather, they emphasise strongly that what the cross was really about was an issue between God and God, the Father and the Son. For these writers, the historical event is just an indirect reflection of a suprahistorical reality that only faith can perceive: Jesus delivered up by the Father to suffer cruelly so that he might expiate in our stead man's offence against the Majesty of God. This theme has been theatricalised by preachers, justified by theologians and endorsed by use of the words 'sacrifice' and 'expiation'. The effect of concentrating on the Father-Son issue to the point of Jesus' being forsaken on the cross has been to focus theological attention onto such great abstract questions as love, justice, sin, expiation, the price to be paid or the debt owed. True, the resulting intellectual constructs were intended to magnify divine love, but this end is obscured from view by the dramatic elements, and what emerges is an implacable divine justice which only the death of an innocent victim can appease. In all this, the event itself in its flesh and blood reality, that is, the event set against the context from which it sprang, ceases to be of any concern. It seems to me to be more in keeping with the texts we have available if we consider Jesus' death as the inevitable consequence of his refusal to use the same weapons of oppression as his enemies. He refused to pray for God to send him twelve legions of angels to support him; in so doing he refused to impose his own point of view, by force, on his enemies. He took this refusal to its logical conclusion since he prayed God to forgive them, that is, not to treat them as they were treating him, with violence. Jesus thus identified himself fully with the rejected since he did not keep in reserve for possible last minute use a force that, in the logic of the line of action his enemies had opened up, would have allowed him to prevail over them. He let himself be nailed to the cross, in the hope and trust that God would justify him in the forgiveness he begged for his murderers. Jesus thus rejects oppressive violence not only by setting himself on the side of the weak, but also by refusing to begin using a similar violence in the name of the weak. For myself, I think it is more fruitful to explore this line of approach to what the cross means than to focus on the Father's summons to the Son: Your life in return for my forgiveness. I suspect that the metaphor which praises the negative way is rooted in and draws its justification from this exchange between Father and Son. To my mind, Jesus' cross signifies that he followed his prophetic commitment right through to the end. The cruel end this brave and innocent commitment led to stresses the power of evil in human history. No force which makes use of evil can overcome evil; nothing shows this more clearly than the never-ending recurrence of oppression of the weak. Jesus' cross does not justify the inhumanity of our world; it reveals it. The cross and the human are not contradictory; they go hand in hand.

CONCLUSION: THE CROSS AS A MANIFESTATION OF THE HUMAN

In majority opinion the cross is not only considered as inhuman; it is also accused of justifying the inhuman, of blessing suffering, being an obstacle on the road to human freedom, encouraging unhealthy ascesis and crushing all joy in living. There are good historical grounds for this accusation, as the Church has frequently endeavoured to devalue life and has based its negative approach on the cross of Jesus. With so many examples to the contrary, to attempt to reconcile the cross with the human may seem sheer folly. It is not just bowing to current fashion or today's dominant ideology? Or lacking the perseverance to go on defending what sets Christianity apart in comparison with the demands of a secularised culture shorn of eschatological hope?

The cross is considered inhuman because it threatens man's harmony and well-being. It is seen as perverted because it prevents him from seeking self-fulfilment without feeling guilty and stops him living life to the full. Because it gives negative situations a positive value in the search for God, and so justifies such things as illness, being downtrodden, being humiliated, irreconcilable conflict and death, the cross appears to be hostile to life; it presents the irrepressible human urge to happiness as

F

something that should be destroyed. Must the human then be sacrificed if God is to be honoured?

Although these accusations are justified by the manipulations the death on the cross has been subjected to over the centuries, and are further strengthened by the stress which has been placed on the ascetic ideal Nietzsche condemned[10], they are not necessarily grounded in the Gospel. Jesus did not die on a cross to prove the truth of the ascetic ideal, to justify or glorify suffering or to denigrate the love of life. He died to show how seriously respect for others and the liberation of the weak should be taken. He died so that justice may come into the world; his violent death bears witness to the inhumanity of our social systems and shows up the illusion of believing that it is possible to live in a secure oasis of happiness and well-being provided one cares nothing for others or allows them to be exploited. Jesus calls the poor blessed not because they are poor, but because they are not oppressors. He calls the persecuted blessed not because they are persecuted, but because they are not persecutors. When the Beatitudes name the weak, the poor, the oppressed as heirs to the Kingdom, they are showing the illogicality of our violent social structures, not justifying suffering and misfortune. The cross pierces our cherished illusion that the human already exists. Whereas what exists is the inhuman; the human has yet to be brought forth, and if its birth is painful, that is because the inhuman besets us from all sides. The inhuman is always nearby, like a lion ready to devour us; the human is a fragile victory. Exploitation is never-ending and ever-new: today's poor may be tomorrow's oppressors if they come to power. There is no island, no State, no regime in which by some magic one can remain free of social violence; no sheltered cell where one can linger in contemplation of one's personal innocence. The cross of Jesus is prophetic: the birth of the human means travail and tears. The human is neither instinctive nor natural; it is the product of a constant effort to master the smouldering violence all human relations conceal.

When the cross is related back to the historical event of the crucifixion, it does not exemplify some ascesis needed to attain the spiritual perfection that approach to God supposedly requires; rather, it shows that the nature of interhuman realtions is such that the innocent, that is, the person who refuses to use violence in order to impose on others his own views or those of his group, is shut out from society. That interhuman relations should allow of this rejection is inhuman. And if ascetics is unconcerned about or reinforces this inhumanity, it is itself inhuman.

The theme of this issue of *Concilium* is 'the human' as the criterion of Christian existence. But what do we mean by 'the human'? The Gospel, being realistic, avoids defining it, but shows up the scandalous nature of social systems where the interplay of human realtions leads to the weak, the defenceless and the innocent being shut out. Jesus' death shines a spotlight on the forces at work in human history: to ignore these forces in the name of so-called humanism is to increase the oppressive weight of the inhuman.

Finally, there is the historical paradox that this approach reveals: the very cross which condemns the inhuman violence of our social structures has been used to reinforce oppression. This inversion of values can be explained in part by the way Jesus' cross was detached from the road which led to it and turned into an abstraction. Jesus himself was made to hold life as worthless and contemptible, whereas he died to go on affirming its value to the end. He valued it highly enough to die in order to prevent it being monopolised by a small minority. He died an outcast because he opted to be on the side of the exploited. When the cross is put back into context, and seen in its historical truth, the meaning it has in the Gospel becomes clear; and then it no longer serves to support the inhuman, but to condemn it.

Translated by Ruth Murphy

Notes

1. Celse *Discours vrai contre les Chrétiens* tr. by L. Rougier (Paris 1965) p. 70. The English translation is taken from Origen *Contra Celsum* tr. by H. Chadwick (Cambridge 1953).
2. *Ibid*. p. 71.
3. *Ibid*. p. 72.
4. *Ibid*. p. 72.
5. Quoted in J. Moltmann *The Crucified God* (London 1974) p. 211.
6. Paris 1975.
7. Tome 19 (Paris 1968) p. 1262.
8. Tome 1 (Paris 1958) p. 231 ff.
9. London 1977.
10. F. Nietzsche *Généalogie de la Morale*, 3 ème dissertation 'Que signifient les idéaux ascétiques' tr. by C. Heim, I. Hildebrand and J. Gratien in *Oeuvres philosophiques complètes* Tome VII (Paris 1971).

Joseph Comblin

Humanity and the Liberation of the Oppressed

1. THE HUMANITY OF THE DEVELOPED NATIONS AND THAT OF THE UNDERDEVELOPED

THE FORM of 'humanism' known in the West, rather than the humanisms it has conceived and developed, stems inevitably from Greek humanism. This in its turn was based on the distinction between Hellenes and Barbarians. The West took up this distinction in the form of one between Christians and Pagans, then between civilized peoples and savages, finally between developed nations and underdeveloped. The true human beings are the Greeks, the Christians, the civilized peoples, the developed nations.

The humanisms of the West are aristocratic and élitist. To be human is to adopt a certain quality of life, which is refined and very expensive to maintain. In order to produce a small number of truly human subjects, a great mass of men have to be condemned to a sub-human condition, forced to work and to give their services virtually free.

There is no doubt that this 'style' of human life, which used to be that of the traditional aristocracy, and is now that of the aristocracy in world terms represented by the middle-classes of the West, is only possible at the expense of the sub-humanisation of the great mass of people. But can one call this style of life, that practised by the Western middle-classes, truly human? Does it really represent the highest point achieved by humanity? Is it not rather a caricature of humanity? Do not its pretensions to the most developed form of humanism rather hide a real void of humanity, a lack of depth and of human density? Can one really be human in any real human sense when one's existence depends on the oppression of great masses of people?

In fact, humanity in the true sense of the word is not to be found among the oppressors, even if they do not know themselves as such, but rather among the victims of oppression. The highest point of the meaning of man has for too long been sought in the highest levels of society. Today we should rather look for it at the lowest levels.

The truest form of humanity is to be found among those men and women who are desperately struggling to safeguard a meaning to being human which society and 'civilisation' are determined to destroy. The purest humanity, surely, is found where men believe despite all visible reality, hope against all hope, and refuse to hate a world that tramples them underfoot. It is on the borderlines of humanity, the frontier

74

situations where human beings are threatened with being reduced to a condition fit for animals, that human dignity is reborn, rises up and affirms itself in the most authentic fashion. This humanity is the more authentic in that it oppresses no one, it does not have to take refuge in ignorance so as not to have to lie to itself and to others. So we should look for humanity among the slaves, the peasants exploited by their masters till they bleed, racked by a pitiless economic system, the workers in the underdeveloped countries—and often in those that call themselves developed—who are exploited, forced to follow a brutal assembly-line pattern if they are not summarily dismissed in case they one day become conscious of their potential strength.

We should look for humanity in all those who have been de-humanised in order to support a developed class which can afford the luxury of a 'humanism'. Humanity has not disappeared from these lowest levels of humanity; no, this is where it shines forth strongest. It shines in the extreme cases: when slave revolts, peasant uprisings, workers' strikes are brutally put down. The 'humanist' élites are ruthless when they feel their privileges threatened. There is no comparison between the pressure from the oppressed masses and the ferocity of their repression in Chile in 1973, in Argentine in 1976, in Nicaragua in 1977-8, in El Salvador and Guatemala at the present time, to quote only some recent examples. Scientific torture is in use in tens of countries at present, and it is the citizens of the developed countries who have worked out its methods and who continue to direct their application. But it is those who are tortured, the peoples who are decimated, who provide the finest examples of 'humanity'.

The oppressed are not beyond humanity. They are simply placed in 'inhuman' situations, but the human being in them reacts. The human being will not allow himself or herself to be destroyed.

The true heroes are not those privileged individuals who can provide themselves with exploits to perform, find adversaries they can defeat in 'fair combat'. The true heroes are those thousands, millions of anonymous men and women who every day have to take up the challenge of a superhuman struggle against forces far superior to themselves, which they never chose to stand up to and which impose on them a yoke too heavy for them to bear. The true heroes are the everyday oppressed who nevertheless manage to salvage the essence of their humanity. No doubt they are coarse and lacking in style. They do not possess all the virtues. But it is among them that the most authentic accents of humanity are to be heard.

The voice of humanity is heard first in the cry of the poor, in the clamour of peoples who refuse to accept domination. The greatest human dignity is that of the slave who refuses to accept his servitude. Jesus reached the height of humanity when, reduced to the condition of a slave, he bore witness to the truth, refused to give in, and died.

Humanity is found too in the daily struggle of the poor to stay clean in the midst of filth, honest in the midst of corruption, and to love in a world that cultivates hate and resentment; to be hospitable, welcoming, open, capable of forgiveness, pity and goodness in a world that rewards aggressiveness and applies the law of the jungle. Today the poorest sections of humanity are the last refuges of faith, of hope, of religion, of the virtues, of solidarity, of selfless love.

2. GOD TAKES SIDES

As for God, he has taken sides, he has taken the side of the poor and the oppressed. God does not know man in the abstract, in general. He did not come to save mankind in general, nor all those individuals who make up the sum total of humanity. There is a religion that sees a relationship between a universal God and a universal humanity: it is the religion of the bourgeoisie. The religion of the Bible is that of the poor. In the Bible there are no 'men'; there are oppressors and oppressed, rich and poor, masters and subjects, learned and ignorant. God chooses: he is on the side of the ignorant, the poor, the subjected. God does not form his people from everyone. He accepts some and rejects others. There is a heaven and a hell.

Aristocratic and bourgeois theologies have always been resistant to the idea of hell. Their instinct is for the universal and universal reconciliation: in this way all forms of domination and repression are relativised, and there is no such thing as really serious oppression since in the end all is annulled.

But the Bible and basic Christian tradition are absolutely clear. Between Lazarus and the rich man at his table a great gulf is fixed and God has made his choice. And Jesus died because he took the part of the lost sheep of Israel against the bad shepherds, the leaders of the people. Jesus chose lepers, paralytics, blind people, sinners, those who were despised and rejected, the excommunicated, the poor, pagans, all who were pushed out of society and regarded as worthless.

'The new man' was not made out of mankind in general, or from the totality of mankind, but from the poor, the working people of Corinth, slaves, little people with no pretensions. God revealed his secrets, the meaning of true men, man who lives in the Spirit, to the uneducated and powerless, those who lived anonymously in the world. As for the rich, it was harder for them to find a true humanity than for a camel to pass through the eye of a needle. They had to give up their privileges, their élitism; cease to belong to their class, renounce their identity and put their goods and their gifts at the service of everyone. In fact, they had to become part of the process of liberating the poor and no longer make their culture and their style the norm to be imposed on everyone.

So God has made a choice from among all possible humanisms. We are no longer in a position to choose. Or rather, we must subject all our humanisms to God's criteria.

God's choice had an immediate consequence. God defines an active humanism: one consisting in liberating the oppressed through means of a history. The liberator is the Spirit, which means that the oppressed are invited to liberate themselves through the power of the Spirit. God's choice becomes a history of liberation, and liberation becomes part of the process of movement in history. The oppressed in their struggle for liberation gain the freedom of the children of God.

The history of liberation has inevitable repercussions on humanisms. It produces a history of humanisms, or, at least, steers it in a particular direction. After God's choice has been made, civilisations can no longer conceive of their humanisms in the same terms as before. Once the cry of the poor and oppressed has been recognised as the voice of God himself, all humanisms are called to give an account of themselves.

3. THE HISTORY OF HUMANISMS

It is significant that Greek humanism was defined in terms of education (*paideia*). It regarded man as a being complete in himself and capable of being fashioned like a work of art. With the help of his tutors, the subject was invited to make himself, to sculpt his own virtues, to transform himself into an accomplished being thanks to his own action on himself. Successive Renaissances have not basically changed this stance. There has been a 'Christian humanism' in which everything is a matter of the relationship between 'God and myself', with the outer world and society itself intervening only in so far as they are reflections of the individual, seen as a 'microcosm'; only in so far as they can serve him or provide him with the theatre for and spectators of his exploits. This humanism knew no history apart from that of the individual. Hence the characteristics of not only classical humanism, but of all the medieval and modern humanisms inspired by it: élitism, individualism, narcissism and ingenuity—ingenuity, because it does not know, or pretends not to know, that it is based on a slave or semi-slave society. It does not know the real nature of the material world and social reality and the immense influence they have on the formation and development of the individual.

Then came bourgeois humanism, which is the current one in developed countries and penetrating deeply into the underdeveloped countries as an ideology designed to make them more easily accept their condition of dependence. Bourgeois humanism is based on the relationship between man and matter. In it, man achieves his true fulfilment in work, that is in transforming the material world in order to produce useful objects. Humanity is affirmed in mastery over the material world: it is sought in science, in technical capacity, in economic rationality. Man imposes himself as man through inventing another way of life in which the conditions are laid down by himself. The superior being is the one who gives himself his way of life. But unfortunately, bourgeois humanism destroys social relationships: the strongest build their empire with the forced labour of the weakest. The difference between the ways of life of the strongest and the weakest is accentuated. As an ideology, bourgeois humanism idolises work. But in reality, it only favours the work of small minorities who hold the key to technology, and subjects itself to the holders of capital, who alone can put this technology to work, while it exploits, destroys, dehumanises the work of the poor masses. It destroys traditional crafts without replacing them with work that dignifies the poor. Finally, it destroys nature and the communion of man with nature which has always been one of the props of the humanism of the poor and the oppressed.

4. THE HUMANISM OF TOMORROW

The present crisis of bourgeois society and its humanism forces us to look in a different direction to find the humanism of tomorrow. Man is called to fulfil himself no longer simply through the self-education of the individual, nor through work, but through building up social relationships. The task we face is that of building a society. Human relationships have been destroyed; society is in tatters: nowhere more so than in the Third World is this wreckage of social relationships at all levels, the consequence of the bourgeois conquest of the world, more in evidence. The true man is the one who is capable of establishing relationships with his likes at all levels: this is his present historical task.

It has become impossible, and it would be a nonsense to try, to re-establish the traditional forms of spontaneous solidarity. Today we need a worked-out solidarity, one studied, willed and dug out with perseverance. Who can really set themselves to the task of remaking a society? Not the ruling classes of present-day society: they only want a qualified democracy, a 'protected' or 'strong' democracy, which will enable them to continue to exercise a *de facto* dictatorship over the masses of the people of the Third World by means of regimes of National Security, such as are to be found on every continent. No, those who will carry out the project of a genuinely human society are to be found among the marginalised masses of the people. A truly human society can only be based on popular organisations. Humanity truly so called is that experienced by the leaders and militants among the poor, the peasants, the workers, the unemployed, particularly in the Third World, who are patiently, heroically building the structures of a new society through organising the unprotected masses. These are the ones who are forging a new human solidarity out of the debris of the old one which has been almost entirely destroyed. They are courageously struggling up the slope of history. They are today the disciples and apostles of the man who took pity on the lost sheep without a shepherd. The truly human man is the one who rounds up the lost sheep, who runs into the hills to bring back one by one those sheep that have strayed away and do not know where to go. They are the heroes of today. If socialism means rebuilding a truly human and brotherly society after the conquest of the world by the bourgeoisie, then it must be said that the humanism of tomorrow can only be socialist. But then the word 'socialism' will have to stop immediately evoking those 'true socialisms' that have only too well assimilated the spirit and aims of bourgeois society.

What does this humanism, which is the humanism of God, consist of? It has five elements: word, freedom, action, people, life.

(a) Word

Animals give out signals and communicate information. Man does the same in a much more complex form. But this is not yet word. The word is in God and is God. And it is given by God. God's word is good news; it is the call that arouses the oppressed, the call to and announcement of action. Or rather, it is God's way of acting among men, since the incarnate Son is the Word translated into human language. So being human means in the first place speaking, that is putting God's gift of the word to work. The word becomes fully human and makes human.

The word makes faith be born, engenders hope and sets the poor in motion. It puts flesh back on dry bones and breathes new life into them. It is a force for introducing newness into the world. It is the strength of the poor: their cry, their clamour calls together and reunites. Information communicates what already exists; the word comes from God, creates anew this new society which is being born among the oppressed of the world.

The truly human word is witness: the speaker is entirely committed to it and takes on its risks. It offends the tribunals and their accompanying police forces, the 'death squadrons', terrorism institutionalised by governments, the risk of 'disappearing'. In this word the speaker speaks God and speaks himself at the same time. This is why he becomes fully human in bearing witness just as Jesus did before his judges.

It is very difficult for the rich to risk everything they have to this point. One has to be poor to risk speaking the truth, to call the oppressed together despite the hostility of the entire system. This is why Christ made himself poor in the extreme, and why the Church itself can only begin to speak when it becomes poor.

If the word is powerful, it is equally vulnerable. It defies the force of arms and is fruitful despite this force, but it has to pay the price of its fruitfulness. Unless the seed die . . . So the truly human humanism is found first in this word which is the good news proclaimed to all the oppressed of the world, all the rejected, all the forgotten.

(b) Freedom

The word creates freedom. God is the word and he creates freedom. He calls it and his call brings it into being. Man becomes man in becoming free. He is not born free; he becomes it by winning his freedom with patience through difficulties. He has to win it back from so many forms of slavery.

The free being is one who is made by himself and not by another, or by a system. One who can carry out his own tasks in which he expresses himself, and is not obliged to carry out tasks for others in which others or a system express themselves. Freedom must include emancipation from what is oppressive in itself, as well emancipation form the dominating forces of nature. But more than that, it consists in emancipation from the forms of slavery that exist in society. It is the foundation of a new type of human relationship, based on reciprocity and fraternity.

Bourgeois freedom is based on the isolation and the security of the individual, on the affirmation of his rights and his strength. Bourgeois freedom is tied to ownership of property and in practice tends to become confused with it. But real freedom is based on voluntary acceptance of a social order in which all are able to participate; it is sharing and mutual services. It is not independence, but mutual dependence.

The only freedom is historical; the only freedom comes from the winning of specific freedoms through destruction of privileges and forms of domination in order to establish an order based on exchange and reciprocity. No one wins specific freedoms through declarations of principles, even if these are enshrined in a Constitution, but through a daily struggle for those changes that can be brought about, through winning new rights for the poor at the expense of the pseudo-rights of the rich.

(c) Action

Man is action, because God is action and gives the power to perform actions. Jesus came to perform actions: to carry out his Father's plan; he is fully man in making God's actions his own.

Man is his deeds. He is not the consciousness he has of himself, not what he thinks himself to be, not what he thinks he has made himself. His actions make him, because they make his true being. This is why man will be judged by his deeds which are his only being. He is found only in his deeds. If he does not act, he is only an illusion of being.

Action is neither internal nor external, but a fusion of internal and external. The highest action was Jesus' death on the Cross, in which the deepest interiority and the most complete exteriority met.

Action contains a modification of the subject by himself. It also contains work, which is modification of the material world. But first and foremost it is transformation of social relationships: action in the fullest sense is the liberation of the oppressed. This is struggle against the existing disorder in order to create new social relationships. This requires all human energies and resources to be brought to bear: in it man develops all his dimensions and becomes truly human.

Action is a struggle 'against': against the established system and also against those who cling to the system and seek to maintain it. But action is above all a struggle 'for': for the unity of all the poor and all the oppressed in a common will. This struggle which is really the fulness of humanity does not seek to replace one power by another, but to create another way of living together. It is the creator of the fulness of human being.

Word and freedom issue in action. This in its turn becomes word and creates freedom: so the movement of liberation feeds on itself in an uninterrupted dynamism.

(d) The people

There is no humanity outside the people. Nothing that remains purely individual can be called human. Faith, hope, thought and action are only valid if they are integrated in a people and experienced in the name of a people for the liberation of a whole people. What I do in my own name has no value; only what I do in the name of all my people.

Not everyone goes to make up the people. The people is not a universal term, any more than the Church embraces the whole of humanity, but on the contrary divides them, just as Jesus divided them. The people is made up of all those who have solidarity with one another. It is made up of the interaction of different strands of solidarity. Those individuals who cut themselves off from all forms of solidarity and make society the setting for their individual affirmation of themselves do not constitute part of the people. They are its adversaries.

In the final analysis, there is only one people, which is the people of God. God did not create 'man' in the abstract, but he created his people and saves through a history. This people is the solidarity and the exchange of all peoples. God speaks to his people. The prophets speak to their peoples. The only free people are peoples and action produces the liberation of these peoples.

The one and only people of God is the ultimate and always present point of reference for what is truly human. If action is directed towards a group lower than this people, there is always a deformation of what is human. The call to all the oppressed, all the poor of the world, all those who are despised and rejected, is the horizon of true humanity.

Nevertheless, a specific person cannot reach the whole of this people except through the instrument of mediations, which can of course always be dangerous when they become closed totalities, but which are nonetheless indispensable.

The first mediation is that of culture and language. The poor can only enter into relationships of dialogue and exchange with others when these base themselves on their territory, their past, the ties they have with those who are close to them. One can only love one's neighbour, those who are close to one, not the whole of humanity in general. Faced with universal empires which impose their own culture, that which reinforces and justifies domination, the poor can only free themselves and exist with the help of their own culture, which they must first protect if they wish to remain what they are and want to be in the face of those who monopolise their whole being. The symbols they hold in common cement a people together and enable it to enter into relationships with other peoples so as to become one people. Among these symbols the religion of the people is naturally the most basic.

In second place, the poor need a social and political mediation. They need to rely on popular organisations and also on their nation. Nationalism is essential to stand up to the great empires. It is through their nations that the poor can make their voice heard in the concert of nations. The dangerous nationalism is that of the great powers; that of the poor nations is a necessary instrument. The poor nations have to rely on their individualities if they are to gain access to true universality. They must unmask the false universal pretensions of the empires that are stronger today than they have ever been.

This is why a complete liberation of what is human has a cultural component and a political one (in the broad sense of anything that relates to the life of a nation). Human man is involved in a cultural struggle and in a political struggle.

(e) Life

Finally, to be human is to love life, to live intensely and to produce life.

Taste for life, respect for life, participation in life in all its dimensions, development of all life's activities: being human is not being one-dimensional but taking part in all that lives, examines itself, expresses itself. Being human means excluding nothing. Furthermore, life is lived with others and being human means constantly multiplying one's relationships with others.

Nevertheless, it is equally human to know how to risk one's life and to lose it in the struggle for life, for liberation. Knowing how to die for life, knowing how to accept one's death and even knowing how to live fully are also aspects of being human.

There is no contradiction between knowing how to live and knowing how to die because a death undergone for liberation opens the gates of eternal life. It is not a question of resigning oneself to death, but of trusting in the ultimate victory of life.

Those who die in large numbers in this way, in long, dark struggles, in witness to life and in the hope of the triumph of life, are the poor of the world: 20,000 in less than two years in El Salvador, thirty-four per day on average in Guatemala in 1980, and more in 1981. Savagely killed by faceless men, with no defences, no arms other than their witness; that of their word, their action, their freedom, their life. In them the people of God lives in the fulness of humanity and the Son of God becomes perfect man.

Translated by Paul Burns

Contributors

JOSEPH COMBLIN was born in Brussels in 1923, and ordained in 1947. He studied theology in Louvain, and has been a parish priest in Belgium, Brazil, and Chile, where he also lectured in theology at the University of Santiago. He taught at Louvain from 1971 to 1980, when he returned to Latin America, where he is active mainly in Brazil and Chile. His recent works translated into English are *The Meaning of Mission* (1977) and *The Church and the National Security State* (1979).

CHRISTIAN DUQUOC, OP, was born in 1926 in Nantes (France) and ordained in 1953. He studied at the University of Friburg (Switzerland), Le Saulchoir (France) and the Ecole Biblique in Jerusalem (Israel). He is a doctor of theology, and teaches dogmatic theology in the Catholic University in Lyons (France). He is on the editorial board of *Lumière et Vie*. His publications include *Christologie*, 2 vols. (1968, 1972), *Jésus, homme libre* (1973) and *Dieu différent* (1977).

PETER EICHER was born in Winterthur, Switzerland, in 1943. He studied philosophy, literature, history and theology at Fribourg and Tübingen, gaining his DPhil in 1969 and his DTheol in 1976. From 1974 to 1977 he was research assistant at Tübingen, and since 1977 he has been professor of systematic theology at Paderborn. He is married with five children. His publications include: *Die anthropologische Wende* (1970); *Solidarischer Glaube* (1975); *Offenbarung – Prinzip neuzeitlicher Theologie* (1977); *Im Verborgenen offenbar* (1978); (ed.) *Gottesvorstellung und Gesellschaftsentwicklung* (1979); *Der Herr gibts den Seinen im Schlaf* (1980); *Theologie – Eine Einführung in das Studium* (1980); and numerous articles.

NORBERT GREINACHER was born in 1931 in Freiburg im Breisgau, Germany. He gained a doctorate in theology in 1955 and was ordained priest in 1956. He is professor of practical theology in the Faculty of Catholic Theology, Tübingen. He has published widely in the following areas: practical theology and the Christian life; the Church and modern society; the priesthood; pastoral sociology; theology and justice; theology and politics; theology and social concerns; liberation theology; Christian rights; the case of Hans Küng. His books thus include the following: *Die Kirche in der Städtischen Gesellschaft* (Mainz 1966); *Angst in der Kirche Verstehen und Überwinden* (Mainz 1972); *Gemeindepraxis – Analysen und Aufgaben* (Munich 1979); *Kirche der Armen Zurtheologie der Befreiung* (Munich 1980); *Der Fall Küng. Eine Dokumentation* (Munich 1980).

JEAN LADRIÈRE teaches at the Catholic University of Louvain, where he directs the Centre for the Philosophy of Sciences. Since 1973 he has been president of the Union Mondiale des Sociétés Catholiques de Philosophie. He has written on the mathematical sciences and the relationship of Christianity, science and society. His most recent works are *Les Enjeux de la rationalité: Le défi de la science et de la technologie aux cultures* (1977) and *Filosofia e práxis científica* (1978).

DIETMAR MIETH was born in Berlin in 1940 and grew up in the Saarland. After gaining a doctorate in theology he lectured in Tübingen, where he presented his professorial thesis. He was professor of moral theology in Fribourg from 1974 to 1981. Since 1981 he has been professor of theological ethics in Tübingen. He has published on Meister Eckhart and on ethics, in such books as *Dichtung, Glaube und Moral* (1976) and *Moral und Ehrfahrung* (1979).

BERNARD QUELQUEJEU, OP, was born in 1932 in Paris. He studied at the Ecole Polytechnique in 1953 and entered the Dominican order in 1957. He qualified in theology at Le Saulchoir and became a doctor of philosophy at the University of Nanterre in 1968. At present he is teaching anthropology and philosophical ethics at the Institut Catholique in Paris and is the editor-in-chief of the *Revue des Sciences philosophiques et théologiques*. His main works include: *La Volonté dans la philosophie de Hegel* (Paris 1972), which was his doctoral thesis; *Une Foi exposée* (Paris 1972), written together with J.-P. Jossua and P. Jacquemont; *Le Temps de la patience. Etude sur le témoignage* (Paris 1976); *De qui tenir. Portraits de famille* (Paris 1979); *Le Manifeste de la liberté chrétienne* (Paris 1976). He has also written many articles on moral and political philosophy, including a series on 'Karl Marx a-t-il constitué une theorie du pouvoir d'Etat?': Iq. 'Le Débat avec Hegel (1841-43)' *RSPT* 63 (1979) 17-60; 2. 'Emancipation humaine et révolution prolétarienne (1844-45)' *ibid.* 63 (1979) 203-240; 3. 'Conquête du pouvoir et fin du politique (1846-48)', *ibid.* 63 (1979) 365-418.

EDWARD SCHILLEBEECKX, OP, was born in Antwerp (Belgium) in 1914 and was ordained in 1941. He studied at Louvain, Le Saulchoir, the Ecole des Hautes Etudes and the Sorbonne (Paris). He bacame a doctor of theology in 1951 and magister in 1959. Since 1958, he has been teaching dogmatic theology and hermeneutics at the University of Nijmegen (the Netherlands). He is editor-in-chief of the Dutch theological review *Tijdschrift voor Theologie*. His works in English translation include: *Christ, the Sacrament of the Encounter with God* (New York 1963); *The Understanding of Faith* (New York and London 1974); *Jesus, An Experiment in Christology* (New York and London 1979); *Christ. The Experience of Jesus as Lord* (New York 1980); *Christ. The Christian Experience in the Modern World* (London 1980); *Jesus and Christ. Interim Report on the Books Jesus and Christ* (New York and London 1980); *Ministry. Leadership in the Community of Jesus Christ* (New York 1981); *Ministry. A Case for Change* (London 1981).

XAVIER THÉVENOT was born in 1938 at Saint-Dizier (France). A Don Bosco Salesian, he was ordained priest in 1968. He teaches moral theology at the Institute Catholique in Paris. The subject of his doctoral thesis in theology was *Homosexualite et moral chretienne*. He is co-author of *Sexualite et vie chretienne, point de vue catholique* (Paris 1981), and has written numerous articles on sexual morality in *Laennec, Etudes, Medecine de l'homme, Prêtres diocesains*.

ANTOON VERGOTE was born in Courtrai (Belgium) in 1921. He received a doctorate in theology in 1950 and in 1954 a doctorate in philosophy at the University of

Louvain. He studied philosophy, psychology and psychoanalysis in Paris. Since 1962 he has been professor in ordinary of religious psychology and religious philosophy at the University of Louvain. In collaboration with W. Huber and H. Piron, he wrote *La Psychanalyse, science de l'homme* (Brussels 1970). This book has been translated into various languages. His book *Psychologie religieuse* (Brussels 1972), has been translated into Dutch, English, German, Italian and Spanish, and was awarded the Frans Van Cauwelaertprijs for 1972. Other publications: *Het huis is nooit af. Gedachten over mens en religie* (Antwerp-Utrecht 1974); *La Teologia e la sua Archeologia. Fede, teologia e scienze umane (Rivelazione e Storia:* 2) (Fossano 1974); *Interprétation du language religieux* (Paris 1974); *Dette et désir. Deux axes chrétiens et la dérive pathologique* (Paris: Editions du Seuil 1978); *Bekentenis en begeerte. Psychoanalytische verkenning van de religie* (translation of *Dette et désir*) (Antwerp-Utrecht 1979); *The Parental Figures and the Representation of God,* with A. Tamayo (Louvain 1980).

CONCILIUM

All back issues are still in print and available for sale. Orders should be sent to the publishers,

T. & T. CLARK LIMITED
36 George Street, Edinburgh EH2 2LQ, Scotland